Joseph Fisher

**The History of Landholding in England**

Joseph Fisher

**The History of Landholding in England**

ISBN/EAN: 9783337338770

Printed in Europe, USA, Canada, Australia, Japan

Cover: Foto ©ninafisch / pixelio.de

More available books at **www.hansebooks.com**

# HUMBOLDT LIBRARY

OF

## POPULAR SCIENCE LITERATURE.

No. 27. Vol. II.]   NEW YORK: J. FITZGERALD & CO.   [FIFTEEN CENTS.

December, 1881.   Entered at the New York Post-Office as Second-Class Matter.   $1.50 per Year (12 Numbers).

## THE HISTORY

OF

## LANDHOLDING IN ENGLAND.

BY JOSEPH FISHER, F.R.H.S.

"Much food is in the tillage of the poor, but there is that is destroyed for want of Judgment."
—PROV. 13:23.

"Of all arts, tillage or agriculture is doubtless the most useful and necessary, as being the source whence the nation derives its subsistence. The cultivation of the soil causes it to produce an infinite increase. It forms the surest resource and the most solid fund of riches and commerce for a nation that enjoys a happy climate. . . . The cultivation of the soil deserves the attention of the Government, not only on account of the invaluable advantages that flow from it, but from its being an obligation imposed by nature on mankind."—VATTEL.

---

### INTRODUCTION.

THIS work is an expansion of a paper read at the meeting of the Royal Historical Society in May, 1875, and will be published in the volume of the Transactions of that body. But as it is an expensive work, and only accessible to the Fellows of that Society, and as the subject is one which is now engaging a good deal of public consideration, I have thought it desirable to place it within the reach of those who may not have access to the larger and more expensive work.

I am aware that much might be added to the information it contains, and I possess materials which would have more than doubled its size, but I have endeavored to seize upon the salient points, and to express my views as concisely as possible.

I have also preferred giving the exact words of important Acts of Parliament to any description of their objects.

If this little essay adds any information upon a subject of much public interest, and contributes to the just settlement of a very important question, I shall consider my labor has not been in vain.    JOSEPH FISHER.

WATERFORD, November 3, 1875.

---

I DO not propose to enter upon the system of landholding in Scotland or Ireland, which appears to me to bear the stamp of the Celtic origin of the people, and which was preserved in Ireland long after it had disappeared in other European countries formerly inhabited by the Celts. That ancient race may be regarded as the original settlers of a large portion of the European continent, and its land system possesses a remarkable affinity to that of the Slavonic, the Hindoo, and even the New Zealand races. It was originally Patriarchal, and then Tribal, and was communistic in its character.

I do not pretend to great originality in my views. My efforts have been to collect the scattered rays of light, and to bring them to bear upon one interesting topic. The present is the child of the past. The ideas of bygone races affect the practices of living people. We form but parts of a whole; we are influenced by those who preceded us, and we shall influence those who come after us. Men cannot disassociate themselves either from the past or the future.

In looking at this question there is, I think, a vast difference which has not been sufficiently recognized. It is the broad distinction between the system arising out of the original occupation of land, and that proceeding out of the necessities of conquest; perhaps I should add a third—the complex system proceeding from an amalgamation, or from the existence of both systems in the same nation. Some countries have been so repeatedly swept over by the tide of conquest that but little of the aboriginal ideas or systems have survived the flood. Others have submitted to a change of governors and preserved their customary laws; while in some there has been such a fusion of the two systems that we cannot decide which of the ingredients was the older, except by a process of analysis and a comparison of the several products of the alembic with the recognized institutions of the class of original or of invading peoples.

Efforts have been made, and not with very great success, to define the principle which governed the more ancient races with regard to the possession of land. While unoccupied or unappropriated, it was common to every settler. It existed for the use of the whole human race. The process by which that which was common to all became the possession of the individual has not been clearly stated. The earlier settlers were either individuals, families, tribes, or nations. In some cases they were nomadic, and used the natural products without taking possession of the land; in others they occupied districts differently defined. The individual was the unit of the family, the patriarch of the tribe. The commune was formed to afford mutual protection. Each sept or tribe in the early enjoyment of the products of the district it selected was governed by its own customary laws. The cohesion of these tribes into states was a slow process; the adoption of a general system of government still slower. The disintegration of the tribal system, and dissolution of the commune, was not evolved out of the original elements of the system itself, but was the effect of conquest; and, as far as I can discover, the appropriation to individuals of land which was common to all, was mainly brought about by conquest, and was guided by impulse rather than regulated by principle.

Mr. Locke thinks that an individual became sole owner of a part of the common heritage by mixing his labor with the land, in fencing it, making wells, or building; and he illustrates his position by the appropriation of wild animals, which are common to all sportsmen, but become the property of him who captures or kills them. This acute thinker seems to me to have fallen into a mistake by confounding *land* with *labor*. The improvements were the property of the man who made them, but it by no means follows that the expenditure of labor on land gave any greater right than to the labor itself or its representative.

It may not be out of place here to allude to the use of the word *property* with reference to land; *property*—from *proprium*, my own—is something pertaining to man. I have a property in myself. I have the right to be free. All that proceeds from myself, my thoughts, my writings, my works, are property; but no man made land, and therefore it is not property. This incorrect application of the word is the more striking in England, where the largest title a man can have is "tenancy in fee," and a tenant holds but does not own.

Sir William Blackstone places the

# THE HISTORY OF LANDHOLDING IN ENGLAND.

possession of land upon a different principle. He says that, as society became formed, its instinct was to preserve the peace; and as a man who had taken possession of land could not be disturbed without using force, each man continued to enjoy the use of that which he had taken out of the common stock; but, he adds, that right only lasted as long as the man lived. Death put him out of possession, and he could not give to another that which he ceased to possess himself.

Vattel (book i., chap. vii.) tells us that "the whole earth is destined to feed its inhabitants; but this it would be incapable of doing if it were uncultivated. Every nation is then obliged by the law of nature to cultivate the land that has fallen to its share, and it has no right to enlarge its boundaries or have recourse to the assistance of other nations, but in proportion as the land in its possession is incapable of furnishing it with necessaries." He adds (chap. xx.), "When a nation in a body takes possession of a country, everything that is not divided among its members remains common to the whole nation, and is called public property."

An ancient Irish tract, which forms part of the Senchus Mor, and is supposed to be a portion of the Brehon code, and traceable to the time of St. Patrick, speaks of land in a poetically symbolic, but actually realistic manner, and says, "Land is perpetual man." All the ingredients of our physical frame come from the soil. The food we require and enjoy, the clothing which enwraps us, the fire which warms us, all save the vital spark that constitutes life, is of the land, hence it is "*perpetual man.*" Selden ("Titles of Honor," p. 27), when treating of the title "King of Kings," refers to the eastern custom of homage, which consisted not in offering the person, but the elements which composed the person, *earth* and *water*—"*the perpetual man*" of the Brehons—to the conqueror. He says:

"So that both titles, those of King of Kings and Great King, were common to those emperors of the two first empires; as also (if we believe the story of Judith) that ceremonies of receiving an acknowledgment of regal supremacy (which, by the way, I note here, because it was as homage received by kings in that time from such princes or people as should acknowledge themselves under their subjection) by acceptance upon their demand of *earth* and *water*. This demand is often spoken of as used by the Persian, and a special example of it is in Darius' letters to Indathyr, King of the Scythians, when he first invites him to the field; but if he would not, then bringing to your sovereign as gifts earth and water, come to a parley. And one of Xerxes' ambassadors that came to demand earth and water from the state of Lacedæmon, to satisfy him, was thrust into a well and earth cast upon him."

The earlier races seem to me, either by reasoning or by instinct, to have arrived at the conclusion that every man was, in right of his being, entitled to food; that food was a product of the land, and therefore every man was entitled to the possession of land, otherwise his life depended upon the will of another. The Romans acted on a different principle, which was "the spoil to the victors." He who could not defend and retain his possessions became the slave of the conqueror, all the rights of the vanquished passed to the victor, who took and enjoyed as ample rights to land as those naturally possessed by the aborigines.

The system of landholding varies in different countries, and we cannot discover any idea of abstract right underlying the various differing systems; they are the outcome of law, the will of the sovereign power, which is liable to change with circumstances. The word *law* appears to be used to express two distinct sentiments; one, the will of the sovereign power, which, being accompanied with a penalty, bears on its face the idea that it may be broken by the individual who pays the penalty: "Thou shalt not eat of the fruit of the tree, for on the day thou eatest thereof thou shalt die," was a law. All laws, whether emanating from an absolute monarch or from the representatives of the majority of a state, are mere expressions of the will of the sovereign power, which may be exacted by force. The second use of the word *law* is a record of our experience—*e.g.*, we see the tides ebb and flow, and conclude it is done in obedience to the will of a sovereign power; but the word in that sense does not imply any violation or any punishment. A distinction must also be drawn between laws and codes; the former existed before the latter. The *lex non scripta* prevailed before letters were invented. Every command of the Decalogue was issued, and punishment followed for its breach, before the existence of the engraved tables. The Brehon code, the Justinian code, the Draconian code, were compilations of existing laws; and the same may be said of the common or customary law of England, of France, and of Germany.

I am aware that recent analytical writers have sought to associate *law* with *force*, and to hold that law is a command, and must have behind it sufficient force to compel submission. These writers find at the outset of their examination, that customary law, the "*Lex non scripta*," existed before force, and that the nomination to sovereign power was the outcome of the more ancient customary law. These laws appear based upon the idea of common good, and to have been supported by the "posse comitatus" before standing armies or state constabularies were formed. Vattel says (book i., chap. ii.), "It is evident that men form a political society, and submit to laws solely for their own advantage and safety. The sovereign authority is then established only for the common good of all the citizens. The sovereign thus clothed with the public authority, with everything that constitutes the moral personality of the nation, of course becomes bound by the moral obligations of that nation and invested with its rights." It appears evident, that customary law was the will of small communities, when they were sovereign; that the cohesion of such communities was a confirmation of the customs of each, that the election of a monarch or a parliament was a recognition of these customs, and that the moral and material *force* or power of the sovereign was the outcome of existing laws, and a confirmation thereof. The application of the united force of the nation could be rightfully directed to the requirements of ancient, though unwritten customary law, and it could only be displaced by legislation, in which those concerned took part.

The duty of the sovereign (which in the United Kingdom means the Crown and the two branches of the legislature) with regard to land, is thus described by Vattel:

"Of all arts, tillage or agriculture is doubtless the most useful and necessary, as being the source whence the nation derives its subsistence. The cultivation of the soil causes it to produce an infinite increase. It forms the surest resource, and the most solid fund of riches and commerce for a nation that enjoys a happy climate. The sovereign ought to neglect no means of rendering the land under his jurisdiction as well cultivated as possible.... Notwithstanding the introduction of private property among the citizens, the nation has still the right to take the most effectual measures to cause the aggregate soil of the country to produce the greatest and most advantageous revenue possible. The cultivation of the soil deserves the attention of the Government, not only on account of the invaluable advantages that flow from it, but from its being an obligation imposed by nature on mankind."

Sir Henry Maine thinks that there are traces in England of the commune or *mark* system in the village communities which are believed to have existed, but these traces are very faint. The subsequent changes were inherent in, and developed by, the various conquests that swept over England; even that ancient class of holdings called "Borough English," are a development of a warlike system, under which each son, as he came to manhood, entered upon the wars, and left the patrimonial lands to the youngest son. The system of gavelkind which prevailed in the kingdom of Kent, survived the accession of William of Normandy, and was partially effaced in the reign of Henry VII. It was not the aboriginal or communistic system, but one of its many successors.

The various systems may have run one into the other, but I think there are sufficiently distinct features to place them in the following order :

1st. The *Aboriginal.*
2d. The *Roman.* Population about 1,500,000.
3d. The *Scandinavian* under the Anglo-Saxon and Danish kings—A.D. 450 to A.D. 1066. The population in 1066 was 2,150,000.
4th. The *Norman,* from A.D. 1066 to A.D. 1154. The population in the latter year was 3,350,000.
5th. The *Plantagenet,* from 1154 to 1485 ; in the latter the population was 4,000,000.
6th. The *Tudor,* 1485 to 1603, when the population was 5,000,000.
7th. The *Stuarts,* 1603 to 1714, the population having risen to 5,750,000.
8th. The *Present,* from 1714. Down to 1820 the soil supported the population ; now about one half lives upon food produced in other countries. In 1874 the population was 23,648,607.

Each of these periods has its own characteristic, but as I must compress my remarks, you must excuse my passing rapidly from one to the other.

### I. THE ABORIGINES.

The aboriginal period is wrapped in darkness, and I cannot with certainty say whether the system that prevailed was Celtic and Tribal. An old French customary, in a MS. treating upon the antiquity of tenures, says : " The first English king divided the land into four parts. He gave one part to the *Arch Flamens* to pray for him and his posterity. A second part he gave to the earls and nobility, to do him knight's service. A third part he divided among husbandmen, to hold of him in socage. The fourth he gave to mechanical persons to hold in burgage." The terms used apply to a much more recent period and more modern ideas.

Cæsar tells us "that the island of Britain abounds in cattle, and the greatest part of those within the country never sow their land, but live on flesh and milk. The sea-coasts are inhabited by colonies from Belgium, which, having established themselves in Britain, began to cultivate the soil."

Diodorus Siculus says, " The Britons, when they have reaped their corn, by cutting the ears from the stubble, lay them up for preservation in subterranean caves or granaries. From thence, they say, in very ancient times, they used to take a certain quantity of ears out every day, and having dried and bruised the grains, made a kind of food for their immediate use."

Jeffrey of Monmouth relates that one of the laws of Dunwalls Molnutus, who is said to have reigned B.C. 500, enacted that the ploughs of the husbandmen, as well as the temples of the gods, should be sanctuaries to such criminals as fled to them for protection.

Tacitus states that the Britons were not a free people, but were under subjection to many different kings.

Dr. Henry, quoting Tacitus, says, " In the ancient German and British nation the whole riches of the people consisted in their flocks and herds ; the laws of succession were few and simple : a man's cattle, at death, were equally divided among his sons ; or, if he had no sons, his daughters ; or if he had no children, among his nearest relations. These nations seem to have had no idea of the rights of primogeniture, or that the eldest son had any title to a larger share of his father's effects than the youngest."

The population of England was scanty, and did not probably exceed a million of inhabitants. They were split up into a vast number of petty chieftainries or kingdoms ; there was no cohesion, no means of communication between them ; there was no sovereign power which could call out and combine the whole strength of the nation. No single chieftain could oppose to the Romans a greater force than that of one of its legions, and when a footing was obtained in the island, the war became one of detail ; it was a provincial rather than a national contest. The brave, though untrained and ill-disciplined warriors, fell before the Romans, just as the Red Man of North America was vanquished by the English settlers.

## II. THE ROMAN.

The Romans acted with regard to all conquered nations upon the maxim, "To the victors the spoils." Britain was no exception. The Romans were the first to discover or create an *estate of uses* in land, as distinct from an estate of possession. The more ancient nations, the Jews and the Greeks, never recognized *the estate of uses*, though there is some indication of it in the relation established by Joseph in Egypt, when, during the years of famine, he purchased for Pharaoh the lands of the people. The Romans having seized upon lands in Italy belonging to conquered nations, considered them public lands, and rented them to the soldiery, thus retaining for the state the estate in the lands, but giving the occupier an estate of uses. The rent of these public lands was fixed at one tenth of the produce, and this was termed *usufruct* —the use of the fruits.

The British chiefs, who submitted to the Romans, were subjected to a tribute or rent in corn ; it varied, according to circumstances, from one fifth to one twentieth of the produce. The grower was bound to deliver it at the prescribed places. This was felt to be a great hardship, as they were often obliged to carry the grain great distances, or pay a bribe to be excused. This oppressive law was altered by Julius Agricola.

The Romans patronized agriculture. Cato says, "When the Romans designed to bestow the highest praise on a good man, they used to say he understood agriculture well, and is an excellent husbandman, for this was esteemed the greatest and most honorable character." Their system produced a great alteration in Britain, and converted it into the most plentiful province of the empire ; it produced sufficient corn for its own inhabitants, for the Roman legions, and also afforded a great surplus, which was sent up the Rhine. The Emperor Julian built new granaries in Germany, in which he stored the corn brought from Britain. Agriculture had greatly improved in England under the Romans.

The Romans do not appear to have established in England any military tenures of land, such as those they created along the Danube and the Rhine ; nor do they appear to have taken possession of the land ; the tax they imposed upon it, though paid in kind, was more of the nature of a tribute than a rent. Though some of the best of the soldiers in the Roman legions were Britons, yet their rule completely enervated the aboriginal inhabitants—they were left without leaders, without cohesion. Their land was held by permission of the conquerors. The wall erected at so much labor in the north of England proved a less effectual barrier against the incursions of the Picts and Scots than the living barrier of armed men which, at a later period, successfully repelled their invasions. The Roman rule affords another example that material prosperity cannot secure the liberties of a people, that they must be armed and prepared to repel by force any aggression upon their liberty or their estates.

"Who will be free, *themselves* must strike the blow."

The prosperous "Britons," who were left by the Romans in possession of the island, were but feeble representatives of those who, under Caractacus and Boadicea, did not shrink from combat with the legions of Cæsar. Uninured to arms, and accustomed to obedience, they looked for a fresh master, and sunk into servitude and serfdom, from which they never emerged. Yet under the Romans they had thriven and increased in material wealth ; the island abounded in numerous flocks and herds ; and agriculture, which was encouraged by the Romans, flourished. This wealth was but one of the temptations to the invaders, who seized not only upon the movable wealth of the natives, but also upon the land, and divided it among themselves.

The warlike portion of the aboriginal inhabitants appear to have joined the Cymri and retired westward. Their system of landholding was non-feudal, inasmuch as each man's land was divided among all his sons. One of the laws of Hoel Dha, King of Wales in the tenth century, decreed "that the youngest son shall have an equal share of the estate with the eldest son, and that when the brothers have divided their father's estate among them, the youngest son shall have the best house with all the office houses ; the implements of husbandry, his father's kettle, his axe for cutting wood, and his knife ; these three last things the father cannot give away by gift, nor leave by his last will to any but his youngest son, and if they are pledged they shall be redeemed." It may not be out of place here to say that this custom continued to exist in Wales ; and on its conquest Edward I. ordained, "Whereas the custom is otherwise in Wales than England concerning succession to an inheritance, inasmuch as the inheritance is partible among the heirs-male, and from time whereof the memory of man is not to the contrary hath been partible, Our Lord the King will not have such custom abrogated, but willeth that inheritance shall remain partible among the heirs as it was wont to be, with this exception that bastards shall from henceforth not inherit, and also have portions with the lawful heirs ; and if it shall happen that any inheritance should hereafter, upon failure of heirs-male, descend to females, the lawful heirs of their ancestors last served thereof. We will, of our especial grace, that the same women shall have their portions thereof, to be assigned to them in our court, although this be contrary to the custom of Wales before used."

The land system of Wales, so recognized and regulated by Edward I., remained unchanged until the reign of the first Tudor monarch. Its existence raises the presumption that the aboriginal system of landholding in England gave each son a share of his father's land, and, if so, it did not correspond with the Germanic system described by Cæsar, nor with the tribal system of the Celts in Ireland, nor with the feudal system subsequently introduced.

The polity of the Romans, which endured in Gaul, Spain, and Italy, and tinged the laws and usages of these countries after they had been occupied by the Goths, totally disappeared in England ; and even Christianity, which partially prevailed under the Romans, was submerged beneath the flood of invasion. Save the material evidence of the footprints of "the masters of the world" in the Roman roads, Roman wall, and some other structures, there is no trace of the Romans in England. Their polity, laws, and language alike vanished, and did not reappear for centuries, when their laws and language were reimported.

I should not be disposed to estimate the population of England and Wales, at the retirement of the Romans, at more than 1,500,000. They were like a flock of sheep without masters, and, deprived of the watch-dogs which overawed and protected them, fell an easy prey to the invaders.

III. THE SCANDINAVIANS.

The Roman legions and the outlying semi-military settlements along the Rhine and the Danube, forming a cordon reaching from the German Ocean to the Black Sea, kept back the tide of barbarians, but the volume of force accumulated behind the barrier, and at length it poured in an overwhelming and destructive tide over the fair and fertile provinces whose weak and effeminate people offered but a feeble resistance to the robust armies of the north. The Romans, under the instruction of Cæsar and Tacitus, had a faint idea of the usages of the people inhabiting the verge that lay around the Roman dominions, but they had no knowledge of the influences that prevailed in "the womb of nations," as Central Europe appeared to the Latins, who saw emerging therefrom hosts of warriors, bearing with them their wives, their children, and their portable effects, determined to win a settlement amid the fertile regions owned and improved by the Romans.

These incursions were not colonization in the sense in which Rome understood it ; they were the migrations of a people, and were as full, as complete, and as extensive as the Israelitish invasion of Canaan—they were more destructive of property, but less fatal to life. These migratory hosts left a desert behind them, and they either gained a settlement or perished. The Roman colonies preserved their connection with the parent stem, and invoked aid when in need; but the barbarian hosts had no home, no reserves. Other races, moving with similar intent, settled on the land they had vacated. These brought their own social arrangements, and it is very difficult to connect the land system established by the aborigines with the system which, after a lapse of some hundreds of years, was found to prevail in another tribe or nation which had occupied the region that had been vacated.

Neither Cæsar nor Tacitus gives us any idea of the habits, or usages of the people who lived north of the Belgæ. They had no notion of Scandinavia nor of Sclavonia. The Walhalla of the north, with its terrific deities, was unknown to them; and I am disposed to think that we shall look in vain among the customs of the Teutons for the basis from whence came the polity established in England by the invaders of the fifth century. The Anglo-Saxons came from a region north of the Elbe, which we call Schleswig-Holstein. They were kindred to the Norwegians and the Danes, and of the family of the sea robbers; they were not Teutons, for the Teutons were not and are not sailors. The Belgæ colonized part of the coast—*i.e.*, the settlers maintained a connection with the mainland; but the Angles, the Saxons, and the Jutes did not colonize, they migrated; they left no trace of their occupancy in the lands they vacated. Each separate invasion was the settlement of a district; each leader aspired to sovereignty, and was supreme in his own domains; each claimed descent from Woden, and, like Romulus or Alexander, sought affinity with the gods. Each member of the Heptarchy was independent of, and owed no allegiance to, the other members; and marriage or conquest united them ultimately into one kingdom.

The primary institutions were moulded by time and circumstance, and the state of things in the eleventh century was as different from that of the fifth as those of our own time differ from the rule of Richard II. Yet one was as much an outgrowth of its predecessor as the other.

Attempts have been made, with considerable ingenuity, to connect races with each other by peculiar characteristics, but human society has the same necessities, and we find great similarity in various divisions of society. At all times, and in all nations, society resolved itself into the upper, middle, and lower classes. Rome had its Nobles, Plebeians, and Slaves; Germany its Edhilingi, Frilingi, and Lazzi; England its Eaorls, Thanes, and Ceorls. It would be equally cogent to argue that, because Rome had three classes and England had three classes, the latter was derived from the former, as to conclude that, because Germany had three classes, therefore English institutions were Teutonic. If the invasion of the fifth century were Teutonic we should look for similar nomenclature, but there is as great a dissimilarity between the English and German names of the classes as between the former and those of Rome.

The Germanic *mark* system has no counterpart in the land system introduced into England by the Anglo-Saxons. If village communities existed in England, it must have been before the invasion of the Romans. The German system, as described by Cæsar, was suited to nomads—to races on the wing, who gave to no individual possession for more than a year, that there might be no home ties. The *mark* system is of a later date, and was evidently the arrangement of other races who permanently settled themselves upon the lands vacated by the older nations. And I may suggest whether, as these lands were originally inhabited by the Celts, the conquerors did not adopt the system of the conquered.

Even in the nomenclature of *Feudalism*, introduced into England in the fifth century, we are driven back to Scandinavia for an explanation. The word *feudal* as applied to land has a Norwegian origin, from which country came Rollo, the progenitor of William the Norman. Pontoppidan ("History of Norway," p. 290) says, "The *Odhall*, right of Norway, and the *Udall*, right of Finland, came from the words '*Odh*,' which signifies *proprietors*, and '*all*,' which means *totum*. A transposition of these syllables makes *all odh*, or *allodium*, which means absolute property. *Fee*, which means stipend or pay, united with *oth*, thus forming *Fee-oth* or *Feodum*, denoting stipendiary property." Wacterus states that the word *allode, allodium*, which applies to land in Germany, is composed of *an* and *lot*—*i.e.*, land obtained by lot.

I therefore venture the opinion that the settlement of England in the fifth and sixth centuries was not Teutonic or Germanic, but SCANDINAVIAN.

The lands won by the swords of all were the common property of all; they were the lands of the people, *Folc-land*; they were distributed by lot at the *Folc-gemot*; they were *Odh-all* lands; they were not held of any superior, nor was there any service save that imposed by the common danger. The chieftans were elected and obeyed, because they represented the entire people. Hereditary right seems to have been unknown. The essence of feudalism *was a life estate*, the land reverted either to the sovereign or to the people upon the death of the occupant. At a later period the monarch claimed the power of confiscating land, and of giving it away by charter or deed; and hence arose the distinction between *Folc-land* and *Boc-land* (the land of the book or charter), a distinction somewhat similar to the *freehold* and *copyhold* tenures of the present day. King Alfred the Great bequeathed "his *Bocland* to his nearest relative; and if any of them have children it is more agreeable to me that it go to those born on the male side." He adds, "My grandfather bequeathed his land on the spear side, not on the spindle side; therefore if I have given what he acquired to any on the female side, let my kinsman make compensation."

The several ranks were thus defined by Athelstane:

"1st. It was whilom in the laws of the English that the people went by ranks, and these were the counsellors of the nation, of worship worthy each according to his condition—'eorl,' 'ceorl,' 'thegur,' and 'theodia.'

"2d. If a ceorl thrived, so that he had fully five hides (600 acres) of land, church and kitchen, bell-house and back gatescal, and special duty in the king's hall, then he was thenceforth of thane-right worthy.

"3d. And if a thane thrived so that he served the king, and on his summons rode among his household, if he then had a thane who him followed, who to the king utward five hides, had, and in the king's hall served his lord, and thence, with his errand, went to the king, he might thenceforth, with his fore oath, his lord represent at various needs, and his and his plant lawfully conduct wheresoever he ought.

"4th. And he who so prosperous a vicegerent had not, swore for himself according to his right or it forfeited.

"5th. And if a 'thane' thrived so that he became an eorl, then was he thenceforth of eorl-right worthy.

"6th. And if a merchant thrived so that he fared thrice over the wide sea by his own means (or vessels), then was he thenceforth of thane-right worthy."

The oath of fealty, as prescribed by the law of Edward and Guthrum, was very similar to that used at a later period, and ran thus:

"Thus shall a man swear fealty: By the Lord, before whom this relic is holy, I will be faithful and true, and love all that he loves, and shun all that he shuns, according to God's law, and according to the world's principles, and never by will nor by force, by word nor by work, do aught of what is loathful to him, on condition that he me keep, as I am willing to deserve, and all that fulfil, that our agreement was, when I to him submitted and chose his will."

The *Odh-all* (noble) land was divided into two classes: the *in-lands*, which were farmed by slaves under *Bailiffs*, and the *out-lands*, which were let to ceorls either for one year or for a term. The rents were usually paid in kind, and were a fixed proportion of the produce. Ina, King of the West Saxons, fixed the rent of ten hides (1200 acres), in the beginning of the eighth century, as follows: 10 casks honey, 12 casks strong ale, 30 casks small ale, 300 loaves bread, 2 oxen, 10 wedders, 10 geese, 20 hens, 10 chickens, 10 cheeses, 1 cask butter, 5 salmon, 20 lbs. forage, and 100 eels. In the reign of Edgar the Peaceable (tenth century), land was sold for about four shillings of the then currency per acre. The Abbot of Ely bought an estate about this time, which was paid for at the rate of four sheep or one horse for each acre.

The freemen (*Liberi Homines*) were a very numerous class, and all were trained in the use of arms. Their *Folcland* was held under the penalty of forfeiture if they did not take the field, whenever required for the defence of the country. In addition, a tax, called Danegeld, was levied at a rate varying from two shillings to seven shillings per hide of land (120 acres); and in 1008, each owner of a large estate, 310 hides, was called on to furnish a ship for the navy.

Selden ("Laws and Government of England," p. 34) thus describes the freemen among the Saxons, previous to the Conquest:

"The next and most considerable degree of all the people is that of the *Freemen*, anciently called *Frilingi*,* or *Free-born*, or such as are born free from all yoke of arbitrary power, and from all law of compulsion, other than what is made by their voluntary consent, for all freemen have votes in the making and executing of the general laws of the kingdom. In the first, they differed from the *Gauls*, of whom it is noted that the *commons* are never called to council, nor are much better than servants. In the second, they differ from many free people, and are a degree more excellent, being adjoined to the lords in judicature, both by advice and power (*consilium et authoritates adsunt*), and therefore those that were elected to that work were called *Comites ex plebe*, and made one rank of *Freemen* for wisdom superior to the rest. Another degree of these were beholden for their riches, and were called *Custodes Pagani*, an honorable title belonging to military service, and these were such as had obtained an estate of such value as that their ordinary arms were a helmet, a coat of mail, and a gilt sword. The rest of the freemen were contented with the name of *Ceorls*, and had as sure a title to their own liberties as the *Custodes Pagani* or the country gentlemen had."

Land was liable to be seized upon for treason and forfeited; but even after the monarchs had assumed the functions of the *Folc-gemot*, they were not allowed to give land away without the approval of the great men; charters were consented to and witnessed in council. "There is scarcely a charter extant," says Chief Baron Gilbert, "that is not proof of this right." The grant of Baldred, King of Kent, of the manor of Malling, in Sussex, was annulled because it was given without the consent of the council. The subsequent gift thereof, by Egbert and Athelwolf, was made with the concurrence and assent of the great men. The kings' charters of escheated lands, to which they had succeeded by a personal right, usually declared "that it might be known that what they gave was their own."

Discussions have at various times taken place upon the question, "Was the land-system of this period *feudal?*" It engaged the attention of the Irish Court of King's Bench, in the reign of Charles I., and was raised in this way: James I. had issued "a commission of defective titles." Any Irish owner, upon surrendering his land to the king, got a patent which reconvened it on him. Wentworth (Lord Stafford) wished to *settle* Connaught, as Ulster had been *settled* in the preceding reign, and, to accomplish it, tried to break the titles granted under "the commission of defective titles." Lord Dillon's case, which is still quoted as an authority, was tried. The plea for the Crown alleged that the honor of the monarch stood before his profit, and as the commissioners were only authorized to issue patents to hold *in capite*, whereas they had given title "to hold *in capite*, by knights' service out of Dublin Castle," the grant was bad. In the course of the argument, the existence of feudal tenures, before the landing of William of Normandy, was discussed, and Sir Henry Spelman's views,

---

* This is a Teutonic, not an Anglo-Saxon term; the Anglo-Saxon word is Thane.

as expressed in the Glossary, were considered. The Court unanimously decided that feudalism existed in England under the Anglo-Saxons, and it affirmed that Sir Henry Spelman was wrong. This decision led Sir Henry Spelman to write his "Treatise on Feuds," which was published after his death, in which he reasserted the opinion that feudalism was introduced into England at the Norman invasion. This decision must, however, be accepted with a limitation; I think there was no separate order of *nobility* under the Anglo-Saxon rule. The king had his councillors, but there appears to have been no order between him and the *Folc-gemot*. The Earls and the Thanes met with the people, but did not form a separate body. The Thanes were country gentlemen, not senators. The outcome of the heptarchy was the Earls or Ealdermen; this was the only order of nobility among the Saxons; they corresponded to the position of lieutenants of counties, and were appointed for life. In 1045 there were nine such officers; in 1065 there were but six. Harold's earldom, at the former date, comprised Norfolk, Suffolk, Essex, and Middlesex; and Godwin's took in the whole south coast from Sandwich to the Land's End, and included Kent, Sussex, Hampshire, Wilts, Devonshire, and Cornwall. Upon the death of Godwin, Harold resigned his earldom, and took that of Godwin, the bounds being slightly varied. Harold retained his earldom after he became king, but on his death it was seized upon by the Conqueror, and divided among his followers.

The Crown relied upon the *Liberi Homines* or freemen. The country was not studded with castles filled with armed men. The *House* of the Thane was an unfortified structure, and while the laws relating to land were, in my view, essentially *feudal*, the government was different from that to which we apply the term *feudalism*, which appears to imply baronial castles, armed men, and an oppressed people.

I venture to suggest to some modern writers that further inquiry will show them that *Folc-land* was not confined to commonages, or unallotted portions, but that at the beginning it comprised all the land of the kingdom, and that the occupant did not enjoy it as owner-in-severalty; he had a good title against his fellow-subjects, but he held under the *Folc-gemot*, and was subject to conditions. The consolidation of the sovereignty, the extension of laws of forfeiture, the assumption by the kings of the rights of the popular assemblies, all tended to the formation of a second set of titles, and *boc-land* became an object of ambition. The same individual appears to have held land by both titles, and to have had greater powers over the latter than over the former.

Many of those who have written on the subject seem to me to have failed to grasp either the *object* or the *genius* of FEUDALISM. It was the device of conquerors to maintain their possessions, and is not to be found among nations, the original occupiers of the land, nor in the conquests of states which maintained standing armies. The invading hosts elected their chieftain, they and he had only a life use of the conquests. Upon the death of one leader another was elected, so upon the death of the allottee of a piece of land it reverted to the state. The *genius* of FEUDALISM was life ownership and non-partition. Hence the oath of fealty was a personal obligation, and investiture was needful before the new feudee took possession. The state, as represented by the king or chieftain, while allowing the claim of the family, exercised its right to select the individual. All the lands were considered *Beneficia*, a word which now means a charge upon land, to compensate for duties rendered to the state. Under this system, the feudatory was a commander, his residence a barrack, his tenants soldiers; it was his duty to keep down the aborigines, and to prevent invasion. He could neither sell, give, nor bequeath his land. He received the surplus revenue as payment for personal service, and thus enjoyed his *benefice*. Judged in this way, I think the feudal system existed before the Norman Conquest. Slavery and serfdom undoubtedly prevailed. The country prospered under the Scandinavians; and, from the great abundance of corn, William of Poitiers calls England "the storehouse of Ceres."

## IV. THE NORMANS.

The invasion of William of Normandy led to results which have been represented by some writers as having been the most momentous in English history. I do not wish in any way to depreciate their views, but it seems to me not to have been so disastrous to existing institutions, as the Scandinavian invasion, which completely submerged all former usages. No trace of Roman occupation survived the advent of the Anglo-Saxons; the population was reduced to and remained in the position of serfs, whereas the Norman invasion preserved the existing institutions of the nation, and subsequent changes were an outgrowth thereof.

When Edward the Confessor, the last descendant of Cedric, was on his deathbed, he declared Harold to be his successor, but William of Normandy claimed the throne under a previous will of the same monarch. He asked for the assistance of his own nobles and people in the enterprise, but they refused at first, on the ground that their feudal compact only required them to join in the defence of their country, and did not coerce them into affording him aid in a completely new enterprise; and it was only by promising to compensate them out of the spoils that he could secure their co-operation. A list of the number of ships supplied by each Norman chieftain appears in Lord Lyttleton's "History of Henry III." vol. i., appendix.

I need hardly remind you that the settlers in Normandy were from Norway, or that they had been expelled from their native land in consequence of their efforts to subvert its institutions, and to make the descent of land hereditary, instead of being divisible among all the sons of the former owner. Nor need I relate how they won and held the fair provinces of northern France—whether as a fief of the French Crown or not, is an open question. But I should wish you to bear in mind their affinity to the Anglo-Saxons, to the Danes, and to the Norwegians, the family of Sea Robbers, whose ravages extended along the coasts of Europe as far south as Gibraltar, and, as some allege, along the Mediterranean. Some questions have been raised as to the means of transport of the Saxons, the Jutes, and the Angles, but they were fully as extensive as those by which Rollo invaded France or William invaded England.

William strengthened his claim to the throne by his military success, and by a form of election, for which there were many previous precedents. Those who called upon him to ascend it alleged "that they had always been ruled by legal power, and desired to follow in that respect the example of their ancestors, and they knew of no one more worthy than himself to hold the reins of government."

His alleged title to the crown, sanctioned by success and confirmed by election, enabled him, in conformity with existing institutions, to seize upon the lands of Harold and his adherents, and to grant them as rewards to his followers. Such confiscation and gifts were entirely in accord with existing usages, and the great alteration which took place in the principal fiefs was more a change of persons than of law. A large body of the aboriginal people had been, and continued to be, serfs or villeins; while the mass of the freemen (*Liberi Homines*) remained in possession of their holdings.

It may not be out of place here to say a few words about this important class, which is in reality the backbone of the British constitution; it was the mainstay of the Anglo-Saxon monarchy; it lost its influence during the civil wars of the Plantagenets, but reasserted its power under Cromwell. Dr. Robertson thus draws the line between them and the vassals:

" In the same manner *Liber homo* is commonly opposed to *Vassus* or *Vassalus*, the former denoting an allodial proprietor, the latter one who held of a superior. These freemen were under an obligation to serve the state, and this duty was considered so sacred that *freemen* were prohibited from entering into holy orders, unless they obtained the consent of the sovereign."

De Lolme, chap. i., sec. 5, says :

" The *Liber homo*, or freeman, has existed in this country from the earliest periods, as well as of authentic as of traditionary history, entitled to that station in society as one of his constitutional rights, as being descended from free parents in contradistinction to ' villains,' which should be borne in remembrance, because the term ' freeman ' has been, in modern times, perverted from its constitutional signification without any statutable authority."

The *Liberi Homines* are so described in the Doomsday Book. They were the only men of honor, faith, trust, and reputation in the kingdom ; and from among such of these as were not barons, the knights did choose jurymen, served on juries themselves, bare offices, and dispatched country business. Many of the *Liberi Homines* held of the king *in capite*, and several were freeholders of other persons in military service. Their rights were recognized and guarded by the 55th William I. ;* it is entitled :

" CONCERNING CHEUTILAR OR FEUDAL RIGHTS, AND THE IMMUNITY OF FREEMEN.

" We will also, and strictly, enjoin and concede that all freemen (*Liberi Homines*) of our whole kingdom aforesaid, have and hold their land and possessions well and in peace, free from every unjust exaction and from Tallage, so that nothing be exacted or taken from them except their free service, which of right they ought to do to us and are bound to do, and according as it was appointed (*statutum*) to them, and given to them by us, and conceded by hereditary right for ever, by the common council (*Folc-gemot*) of our whole realm aforesaid."

These freemen were not created by the Norman Conquest, they existed prior thereto ; and the laws, of which this is one, are declared to be the laws of Edward the Confessor, which William re-enacted. Selden, in " The Laws and Government of England," p. 34, speaks of this law as the first Magna Charta. He says :

" Lastly, the one law of the kings, which may be called the first *Magna Charta* in the Norman times (55 William I.), by which the king reserved to himself, from the *freemen* of this kingdom, nothing but their free service, in the conclusion saith that their lands were thus granted to them in inheritance of the king by the *Common Council* (*Folc-gemot*) of the whole kingdom ; and so asserts, in one sentence, the liberty of the freemen, and of the representative body of the kingdom."

He further adds :

" The freedom of an *Englishman* consisteth of three particulars : first, in *ownership ;* second, in *voting any law*, whereby ownership is maintained ; and, thirdly, in having an influence upon the *judiciary power* that must apply the law. Now the English, under the Normans, enjoyed all this freedom with each man's own particular, besides what they had in bodies aggregate. This was the meaning of the Normans, and they published the same to the world in a fundamental law, whereby is granted that all *freemen* shall have and hold their lands and possessions in hereditary right for ever ; and by this they being secured from forfeiture, they are further saved from all wrong by the same law, which provideth that they shall hold them well or quietly, and in peace, free from all unjust tax, and from all Tallage, so as nothing shall be exacted nor taken but their *free service*, which, by right, they are bound to perform."

This is expounded in the law of Henry I., cap. 4, to mean that no tribute or tax shall be taken but what was due in the Confessor's time, and Edward II. was sworn to observe the laws of the Confessor.

The nation was not immediately settled. Rebellions arose either from the oppression of the invaders or the restlessness of the conquered ; and, as each outburst was put down by force, there were new lands to be distributed among

---

* "LV.—De Chartilari seu Feudorum jure et Ingenuorum immunitate. Volumus etiam ac firmiter præcipimus et concedimus ut omnes liberī homines totius Monarchiæ regni nostri prædicti habeant et teneant terras suas et possessiones suas bene et in pace, liberi ab omni, exactione iniusta et ab omni Tallagio : Ita quod nihil ab eis exigatur vel capiatur nisi servicium suum liberum quod de iure nobis facere debent et facere tenentur et prout statutum est eis et illis a nobis datum et concessum iure hæreditario imperpetuum per commune consilium totius regni nostri præicti."

the adherents of the monarch; ultimately there were about 700 chief tenants holding *in capite*, but the nation was divided into 60,215 knights' fees, of which the Church held 28,115. The king retained in his own hands 1422 manors, besides a great number of forests, parks, chases, farms, and houses, in all parts of the kingdom; and his followers received very large holdings.

Among the Saxon families who retained their land was one named Shobington in Bucks. Hearing that the Norman lord was coming to whom the estate had been gifted by the king, the head of the house armed his servants and tenants, preparing to do battle for his rights; he cast up works, which remain to this day in grassy mounds, marking the sward of the park, and established himself behind them to await the despoiler's onset. It was the period when hundreds of herds of wild cattle roamed the forest lands of Britain, and, failing horses, the Shobingtons collected a number of bulls, rode forth on them, and routed the Normans, unused to such cavalry. William heard of the defeat, and conceived a respect for the brave man who had caused it; he sent a herald with a safe conduct to the chief, Shobington, desiring to speak with him. Not many days after, came to court eight stalwart men riding upon bulls, the father and seven sons. "If thou wilt leave me my lands, O king," said the old man, "I will serve thee faithfully as I did the dead Harold." Whereupon the Conqueror confirmed him in his ownership, and named the family Bullstrode, instead of Shobington.

Sir Martin Wright, in his "Treatise on Tenures," published in 1730, p. 61, remarks:

" Though it is true that the possessions of the Normans were of a sudden very great, and that they received most of them from the hands of William I., yet it does not follow that the king took all the lands of England out of the hands of their several owners, claiming them as his spoils of war, or as a parcel of a conquered country; but, on the contrary, it appears pretty plain from the history of those times that the king either had or pretended title to the crown, and that his title, real or pretended, was established by the death of Harold, which amounted to an unquestionable judgment in his favor. He did not therefore treat his opposers as enemies, but as traitors, agreeably to the known laws of the kingdom which subjected traitors not only to the loss of life but of all their possessions."

He adds (p. 63):

" As William I. did not claim to possess himself of the lands of England as the spoils of conquest, so neither did he tyrannically and arbitrarily subject them to feudal dependence; but, as the fedual law was at that time the prevailing law of Europe, William I., who had always governed by this policy, might probably recommend it to our ancestors as the most obvious and ready way to put them upon a footing with their neighbors, and to secure the nation against any future attempts from them. We accordingly find among the laws of William I. a law enacting feudal law itself, not *eo nomine*, but in effect, inasmuch as it requires from all persons the same engagements to, and introduces the same dependence upon, the king as supreme lord of all the lands of England, as were supposed to be due to a supreme lord by the feudal law. The law I mean is the LII. law of William I."

This view is adopted by Sir William Blackstone, who writes (vol. ii., p. 47):

" From the prodigious slaughter of the English nobility at the battle of Hastings, and the fruitless insurrection of those who survived, such numerous forfeitures had accrued that he (William) was able to reward his Norman followers with very large and extensive possessions, which gave a handle to monkish historians, and such as have implicitly followed them, to represent him as having, by the right of the sword, seized upon all the lands of England, and dealt them out again to his own favorites— a supposition grounded upon a mistaken sense of the word conquest, which 'in its feudal acceptation signifies no more than acquisition, and this has led many hasty writers into a strange historical mistake, and one which, upon the slightest examination, will be found to be most untrue.

" We learn from a Saxon chronicle (A.D. 1085), that in the nineteenth year of King William's reign, an invasion was apprehended from Denmark; and the military constitution of the Saxons being then laid aside, and no other introduced in its stead, the kingdom was wholly defenceless; which occasioned the king to bring over a large army of Normans and Britons, who were quartered upon, and greatly oppressed, the people. This apparent weakness, together with the grievances occasioned by a foreign force, might co-operate with the king's remonstrance, and better incline the nobility to listen to his proposals for putting them in a position of defence. For, as soon as the danger was over, the king held a great council to inquire into the state of the nation, the immediate consequence of which was the compiling of the great survey called the Doomsday Book, which was finished the next year; and in the end of that very year (1086) the king was attended by all his nobility at Sarum, where the principal landholders submitted their lands to the yoke of military tenure, and became the king's vassals, and did homage and fealty to his person."

Mr. Henry Hallam writes:

"One innovation made by William upon the feudal law is very deserving of attention. By the leading principle of feuds, an oath of fealty was due from the vassal to the lord of whom he immediately held the land, and no other. The King of France long after this period had no feudal, and scarcely any royal, authority over the tenants of his own vassals; but William received at Salisbury, in 1085, the fealty of all landholders in England, both those who held in chief and their tenants, thus breaking in upon the feudal compact in its most essential attribute—the exclusive dependence of *a vassal* upon his lord; and this may be reckoned among the several causes which prevented the continental notions of independence upon the Crown from ever taking root among the English aristocracy."

A more recent writer, Mr. Freeman ("History of the Norman Conquest," published in 1871, vol. iv., p. 695), repeats the same idea, though not exactly in the same words. After describing the assemblage which encamped in the plains around Salisbury, he says:

"In this great meeting a decree was passed, which is one of the most memorable pieces of legislation in the whole history of England. In other lands where military tenure existed, it was beginning to be held that he who plighted his faith to a lord, who was the man of the king, was the man of that lord only, and did not become the man of the king himself. It was beginning to be held that if such a man followed his immediate lord to battle against the common sovereign, the lord might draw on himself the guilt of treason, but the men that followed him would be guiltless. William himself would have been amazed if any vassal of his had refused to draw his sword in a war with France on the score of duty toward an over-lord. But in England, at all events, William was determined to be full king over the whole land, to be immediate sovereign and immediate lord of every man. A statute was passed that every *freeman* in the realm should take the oath of fealty to King William."

Mr. Freeman quotes Stubbs's "Select Charters," p. 80, as his authority. Stubbs gives the text of that charter, with ten others. He says: "These charters are from 'Textus Roffensis,' a manuscript written during the reign of Henry I.; it contains the sum and substance of all the legal enactments made by the Conqueror independent of his confirmation of the earlier laws." It is as follows: "Statuimus etiam ut *omnis liber homo* feodere et sacramento affirmet, quod intra et extra Angliam Willelmo regi fideles esse volunt, terras et honorem illius omni fidelitate cum eo servare et eum contra inimicos defendere."

It will be perceived that Mr. Hallam reads *Liber homo* as "vassal." Mr. Freeman reads them as "freeman," while the older authority, Sir Martin Wright, says: "I have translated the words *Liberi Homines*, 'owners of land,' because the sense agrees best with the tenor of the law."

The views of writers of so much eminence as Sir Martin Wright, Sir William Blackstone, Mr. Henry Hallam, and Mr. Freeman, are entitled to the greatest respect and consideration, and it is with much diffidence I venture to differ from them. The three older writers appear to have had before them the LII. of William I., the latter the alleged charter found in the "Textus Roffensis;" but as they are almost identical in expression, I treat the latter as a copy of the former, and I do not think it bears out the interpretation sought to be put upon it—that it altered either the feudalism of England, or the relation of the vassal to his lord; and it must be borne in mind that not only did William derive his title to the crown from Edward the Confessor, but he preserved the apparent continuity, and re-enacted the laws of his predecessor.

Wilkins' "Laws of the Anglo-Saxons and Normans," republished in 1840 by the Record Commissioners, gives the following introduction:

"Here begin the laws of Edward, the glorious king of England.

"After the fourth year of the succession to the kingdom of William of this land, that is England, he ordered all the English noble and wise men and acquainted with the law, through the whole country, to be summoned before his council of barons, in order to be acquainted with their customs. Having therefore selected from all the counties twelve, they were sworn solemnly to proceed as diligently as they might to write their laws and customs, nothing omitting, nothing adding, and nothing changing."

Then follow the laws, thirty-nine in number, thus showing the continuity of system, and proving that William imposed upon his Norman followers the laws of the Anglo-Saxons. They do not include the LII. William I., to which I shall refer hereafter. I may, however, observe that the demonstration at Salisbury was not of a legislative character; and that it was held in conformity with Anglo-Saxon usages. If, according to Stubbs, the ordinance was a charter, it would proceed from the king alone. The idea involved in the statements of Sir Martin Wright, Mr. Hallam, and Mr. Freeman, that the *vassal of a lord* was then called on to swear allegiance to the *king*, and that it altered the feudal bond in England, is not supported by the oath of vassalage. In swearing fealty, the vassal knelt, placed his hands between those of his lord's, and swore:

"I become your man from this day forward, of life and limb, and of earthly worship, and unto you shall be true and faithful, and bear you faith for the tenements at that I claim to hold of you, *saving the faith that I owe unto our Sovereign Lord the King.*"

This shows that it was unnecessary to call *vassals* to Salisbury to swear allegiance. The assemblage was of the same nature and character as previous meetings. It was composed of the *Liberi Homines*, the freemen, described by the learned John Selden (*ante*, p. 10), and by Dr. Robertson and De Lolme (*ante*, pp. 12, 13).

But there is evidence of a much stronger character, which of itself refutes the views of these writers, and shows that the Norman system, at least during the reign of William I., was a continuation of that existing previous to his succession to the throne; and that the meeting at Salisbury, so graphically portrayed, did not effect that radical change in the position of English landholders which has been stated. I refer to the works of EADMERUS; he was a monk of Canterbury who was appointed Bishop of St. Andrews, and declined or resigned the appointment because the King of Scotland refused to allow his consecration by the Archbishop of Canterbury. His history includes the reigns of William I., William II., and Henry I., from 1066 to 1122, and he gives, at page 173, the laws of Edward the Confessor, which William I. gave to England; they number seventy-one, including the LII. law quoted by Sir Martin Wright. The introduction to these laws is in Latin and Norman-French, and is as follows:

"These are the laws and customs which King William granted to the whole people of England after he had conquered the land, and they are those which *King Edward his predecessor* observed before him."*

This simple statement gets rid of the theory of Sir Martin Wright, of Sir

---

\* The laws of William are given in a work entitled "Eadmeri Monachi Cantuariensis Historia Novorum," etc. It includes the reigns of William I. and II., and Henry I., from 1066 to 1122, and is edited by John Selden. Page 173 has the following:

| "Hæ sunt Leges et Consuetudines quas Willielmus Rex concessit universo Populo Angliæ post subactam terram. Eædum sunt qnas Edwardus Rex cognatus ejus obseruauit ante cum. | "Ces sont les Leis et Custums que le Rui William granted a tut le peuple de Engleterre apres le Conquest de le Terre. Ice les meismes que le Rui Edward sun Cosin tult devant lui. |
|---|---|

" LII.

" De fide et obsequio erga Regnum.

" Statuimus etiam ut *omnes liberi homines* foedere et sacramento affirment quod intra et extra universum regnum Angliæ (quod olim vocabatur regnum Britanniæ) Willielmo suo domino fideles esse volunt, terras et honores illius fidelitate ubique servare cum eo et contra inimicos et alienigenas defendere."

William Blackstone, of Mr. Hallam, and of Mr. Freeman, that William introduced a new system, and that he did so either as a new feudal law or as an amendment upon the existing feudalism. The LII. law, quoted by Wright, is as follows:

"We have decreed that all *free men* should affirm on oath, that both within and without the whole kingdom of England (which is called Britain) they desire to be faithful to William their lord, and everywhere preserve unto him his land and honors with fidelity, and defend them against all enemies and strangers."

Eadmerus, who wrote in the reign of Henry I., gives the LII. William I. as a confirmatory law. The charter given by Stubbs is a contraction of the law given by Eadmerus. The former uses the words *Omnes liberi homines;* the latter, the words *Omnis liber homo.* Those interested can compare them, as I shall give the text of each side by side.

Since the paper was read, I have met with the following passage in Stubbs's "Constitutional History of England," vol. i., p. 265:

"It has been maintained that a formal and definitive act, forming the initial point of the feudalization of England, is to be found in a clause of the laws, as they are called, of the Conqueror, which directs that every freeman shall affirm, by covenant and oath, that 'he will be faithful to King William within England and without, will join him in preserving his land with all fidelity, and defend him against his enemies.' But this injunction is little more than the demand of the oath of allegiance taken to the Anglo-Saxon kings, and is here required not of every feudal dependant of the king, but of every freeman or freeholder whatsoever. In that famous Council of Salisbury, A.D. 1086, which was summoned immediately after the making of the Doomsday survey, we learn, from the 'Chronicle,' that there came to the king 'all his witan and all the landholders of substance in England, whose vassals soever they were, and they all submitted to him and became his men, and swore oaths of allegiance that they would be faithful to him against all others.' In the act has been seen the formal acceptance and date of the introduction of feudalism, but it has a very different meaning. The oath described is the oath of allegiance, combined with the act of homage, and obtained from all landowners whoever their feudal lord might be. It is a measure of precaution taken against the disintegrating power of feudalism, providing a direct tie between the sovereign and all freeholders which no inferior relations existing between them and the mesne lords would justify them in breaking."

I have already quoted from another of Stubbs's works, "Select Charters," the charter which he appears to have discovered bearing upon this transaction, and now copy the note, giving the authorities quoted by Stubbs, with reference to the above passage. He appears to have overlooked the complete narration of the alleged laws of William I., given by Eadmerus, to which I have referred. The note is as follows:

"Ll. William I., § 2, below note; see Hovenden, ii., pref. p. 5, *seq.*, where I have attempted to prove the spuriousness of the document called the Charter of William I., printed in the ancient 'Laws,' ed. Thorpe, p. 211. The way in which the regulation of the Conqueror here referred to has been misunderstood and misused is curious. Lambarde, in the 'Archaionomia,' p. 170, printed the false charter in which this genuine article is incorporated as an appendix to the French version of the Conqueror's laws, numbering the clauses 51 to 67; from Lambarde, the whole thing was transferred by Wilkins into his collection of Anglo-Saxon laws. Blackstone's 'Commentary,' ii. 49, suggested that perhaps the very law (which introduced feudal tenures) thus made at the Council of Salisbury is that which is still extant and couched in these remarkable words, *i.e.*, the injunction in question referred to by Wilkins, p. 228. Ellis, in the introduction to 'Doomsday,' i. 16, quotes Blackstone, but adds a reference to Wilkins, without verifying Blackstone's quotation from his collection of laws, substituting for that work the Concilia, in which the law does not occur. Many modern writers have followed him in referring the enactment of the article to the Council of Salisbury. It is well to give here the text of both passages; that in the laws runs thus: 'Statuimus etiam ut omnis liber homo foedere et sacramento affirmet, quod intra et extra Angliam Willelmo regi fideles esse volunt, terras et honorem illius omni fidelitate eum eo servare et ante eum contra inimicos defendere' (Select Charters, p. 80). The homage done at Salisbury is described by Florence thus: 'Nec multo post mandavit ut Archiepiscopi, episcopi, abbates, comitas et barones et vicecomitas cum suis militibus die Kalendarum Augustarem sibi occurent Saresberiæ quo cum venissent milites eorem sibi fidelitatem contra omnes homines jurare coegit.' The 'Chronicle' is a little more full: 'Thæ him comon to his witan and ealle tha Landsittende men the ahtes wæron ofer eall Engleland wæron thæs mannes men the hi wæron and ealle hi bugon to him and wæron his men, and him hold athas sworon thæt he woldon ongean ealle other men him holde beon.'"

Mr. Stubbs had, in degree, adopted the view at which I had arrived, that the law or charter of William I. was an injunction to enforce the oath of allegiance, previously ordered by the laws of Edward the Confessor, to be taken by all freemen, and that it did not relate to vassals, or alter the existing feudalism.

As the subject possesses considerable interest for the general reader as well as the learned historian, I think it well to place the two authorities side by side, that the text may be compared:

LII. *William I., as given by Eadmerus.*
"De fide et obsequio erga Regnum.
"Statuimus etiam ut *omnes liberi homines foedere* et sacramento affirment quod intra et extra universum regnum Angliæ (quod olim vocabatur regnum Britanniæ) Willielmo suo domino fideles esse volunt, terras et honores illius fidelitate unique servare cum eo et contra inimicos et alienigenas defendere."

*Charter from Textus Roffensis, given by Mr. Stubbs.*
"Statuimus etiam ut *omnis liber homo* feodere et sacramento affirmet, quod intra et extra Angliam Willelmo regi fideles esse volunt, terras et honorem illius omni fidelitate cum eo servare et ante cum contra inimicos defendere."

I think the documents I have quoted show that Sir Martin Wright, Sir William Blackstone, and Messrs. Hallam and Freeman, labored under a mistake in supposing that William had introduced or imposed a new feudal law, or that the vassals of a lord swore allegiance to the king. The introduction to the laws of William I. shows that it was not a new enactment, or a Norman custom introduced into England, and the law itself proves that it relates to freemen, and not to vassals.

The misapprehension of these authors may have arisen in this way: William I. had two distinct sets of subjects. The NORMANS, who had taken the oath of allegiance on obtaining investiture, and whose retinue included vassals; and the ANGLO-SAXONS, among whom vassalage was unknown, who were freemen (*Liberi Homines*) as distinguished from serfs. The former comprised those in possession of Odhal (noble) land, whether held from the Crown or its tenants. It was quite unnecessary to convoke the Normans and their vassals, while the assemblage of the Saxons —*Omnes Liberi Homines*—was not only in conformity with the laws of Edward the Confessor, but was specially needful when a foreigner had possessed himself of the throne.

I have perhaps dwelt too long upon this point, but the error to which I have referred has been adopted as if it was an unquestioned fact, and has passed into our school-books and become part of the education given to the young, and therefore it required some examination.

I believe that a very large portion of the land in England did not change hands at that period, nor was the position of either *serfs* or *villeins* changed. The great alteration lay in the increase in the quantity of *boc-land*. Much of the *folc-land* was forfeited and seized upon, and as the king claimed the right to give it away, it was called *terra regis*. The charter granted by King William to Alan Fergent, Duke of Bretagne, of the lands and towns, and the rest of the inheritance of Edwin, Earl of Yorkshire, runs thus:

" Ego Guilielmus cognomine Bastardus, Rex Angliæ do et concedo tibi nepoti meo Alano Brittaniæ Comiti et hæredibus tuis imperpetuum omnes villas et terras quæ nuper fuerunt Comitis Edwini in Eborashina cum feodis militiæ et aliis libertatibus et consuetudinibus ita libere et honorifice sicut idem Edwinus eadem tenuit.
" Data obsidione coram civitate Eboraci."

This charter does not create a different title, but gives the lands as held by the former possessor. The monarch assumed the function of the *folc-gemot*, but the principle remained—the feudee only became tenant for life. Each estate reverted to the Crown on the death of him who held it; but, previous to acquiring possession, the new tenant had to cease to be his own " man," and became the "man" of his superior. This act was called "homage," and was followed by "investiture." In A.D. 1175, Prince Henry refused to trust himself with his father till his homage had been renewed and accepted, for it bound the superior to protect the inferior. The process is thus described by De Lolme (chap. ii., sec. 1):

"On the death of the ancestor, lands holden by 'knight's service' and by 'grand sergeantcy' were, upon inquisition finding the tenure and the death of the ancestor, seized into the king's hands. If the heir appeared by the inquisition to be within the age of twenty-one years, the king retained the lands till the heir attained the age of twenty-one, for his own profit, maintaining and educating the heir according to his rank. If the heir appeared by the inquisition to have attained twenty-one, he was entitled to demand livery of the lands by the king's officers on paying a relief and doing fealty and homage. The minor heir attaining twenty-one, and proving his age, was entitled to livery of his lands, on doing fealty and homage, without paying any relief."

The idea involved is, that the lands were *held*, and *not owned*, and that the proprietary right lay in the nation, as represented by the king. If we adopt the poetic idea of the Brehon code, that "land is perpetual man," then *homage* for land was not a degrading institution. But it is repugnant to our ideas to think that any man can, on any ground, or for any consideration, part with his manhood, and become by homage the "man" of another.

The Norman chieftains claimed to be peers of the monarch, and to sit in the councils of the nation, as barons-by-tenure and not by patent. This was a decided innovation upon the usages of the Anglo-Saxons, and ultimately converted the Parliament, the *folc-gemot*, into two branches. Those who accompanied the king stood in the same position as the companions of Romulus, they were the *patricians*; those subsequently called to the councils of the sovereign by patent corresponded with the Roman *nobiles*. No such patents were issued by any of the Norman monarchs. But the insolence of the Norman nobles led to the attempt made by the successors of the Conqueror to revive the Saxon earldoms as a counterpoise. The weakness of Stephen enabled the greater feudees to fortify their castles, and they set up claims against the Crown, which aggravated the discord that arose in subsequent reigns.

The "Saxon Chronicles," p. 238, thus describes the oppressions of the nobles, and the state of England in the reign of Stephen:

"They grievously oppressed the poor people with building castles, and when they were built, filled them with wicked men, or rather devils, who seized both men and women who they imagined had any money, threw them into prison, and put them to more cruel tortures than the martyrs ever endured; they suffocated some in mud, and suspended others by the feet, or the head, or the thumbs, kindling fires below them. They squeezed the heads of some with knotted cords till they pierced their brains, while they threw others into dungeons swarming with serpents, snakes, and toads."

The nation was mapped out, and the owners' names inscribed in the Doomsday Book. There were no unoccupied lands, and had the possessors been loyal and prudent, the sovereign would have had no lands, save his own private domains, to give away, nor would the industrious have been able to become tenants-in-fee. The alterations which have taken place in the possession of land since the composition of the Book of Doom, have been owing to the disloyalty or extravagance of the descendants of those then found in possession.

Notwithstanding the vast loss of life in the contests following upon the invasion, the population of England increased from 2,150,000 in 1066, when William landed, to 3,350,000 in 1152, when the great-grandson of the Conqueror ascended the throne, and the first of the Plantagenets ruled in England.

V. THE PLANTAGENETS.

Whatever doubts may exist as to the influence of the Norman Conquest upon the mass of the people—the freemen, the ceorls, and the serfs—there can be no doubt that its effect upon the higher classes was very great. It added to the existing *feudalism*—the system of Baronage, with its concomitants of castellated residences filled with armed men. It led to frequent contests between neighboring lords, in which the liberty and rights of the freemen were imperilled. It also eventuated in the formation of a distinct order—the peerage—and for a time the constitutional influence of the assembled people, the *folc-gemot*, was overborne.

The principal Norman chieftains were barons in their own country, and they retained that position in England, but their holdings in both were feudal, not hereditary. When the Crown, originally elective, became hereditary, the barons sought to have their possessions governed by the same rule, to remove them from the class of *terra-regis* (folc-land), and to convert them into chartered land. Being gifts from the monarch, he had the right to direct the descent, and all charters which gave land to a man and his heirs, made each of them only a tenant for life ; the possessor was bound to hand over the estate undivided to the heir, and he could neither give, sell, nor bequeath it. The land was *beneficia*, just as appointments in the Church, and reverted, as they do, to the patron to be re-granted. They were held upon military service, and the major barons, adopting the Saxon title Earl, claimed to be *peers* of the monarch, and were called to the councils of the state as barons-by-tenure. In reply to a *quo warranto*, issued to the Earl of Surrey, in the reign of Edward I., he asserted that his ancestors had assisted William in gaining England, and were equally entitled to a share of the spoils. "It was," said he, "by their swords that his ancestors had obtained their lands, and that by his he would maintain his rights." The same monarch required the Earls of Hereford and Norfolk to go over with his army to Guienne, and they replied, "The tenure of our lands does not require us to do so, unless the king went in person." The king insisted ; the earls were firm. "By God, sir Earl," said Edward to Hereford, "you shall go or hang." "By God, sir King," replied the earl, "I will neither go nor hang." The king submitted and forgave his warmth.

The struggle between the nobles and the Crown commenced, and was continued, under varying circumstances. Each of the barons had a large retinue of armed men under his own command, and the Crown was liable to be overborne by a union of ambitious nobles. At one time the monarch had to face them at Runnymede and yield to their demands ; at another he was able to restrain them with a strong hand. The Church and the barons, when acting in union, proved too strong for the sovereign, and he had to secure the alliance of one of these parties to defeat the views of the other. The barons abused their power over the *freemen*, and sought to establish the rule "that every man must have a lord," thus reducing them to a state of vassalage. King John separated the barons into two classes— major and minor ; the former should have at least thirteen knights' fees and a third part ; the latter remained country gentlemen. The 20th Henry III., cap. 3 and 4, was passed to secure the rights of freemen, who were disturbed by the great lords, and gave them an appeal to the king's courts of assize.

Bracton, an eminent lawyer who wrote in the time of Henry III., says :

"The king hath superiors—viz., God and the law by which he is made king ; also his court — viz., his earls and barons. Earls are the king's associates, and he that hath an associate hath a master ; and therefore, if the king be unbridled, or (which is all one) without law, they ought to bridle him, unless they will be unbridled as the king, and then the commons may cry, Lord Jesus, pity us," etc.

An eminent lawyer, time of Edward I., writes :

"Although the king ought to have no equal in the land, yet because the king and his commissioners can be both judge and party, the king ought by right to have companions, to hear and determine in Parliament all writs and plaints of wrongs done by the king, the queen, or their children."

# THE HISTORY OF LANDHOLDING IN ENGLAND.

These views found expression in the coronation oath. Edward II. was forced to swear:

"Will you grant and keep, and by your oath confirm to the people of England the laws and customs to them, granted by the ancient kings of England, your righteous and godly predecessors; and especially to the clergy and people, by *the glorious King St. Edward*, your predecessor?"
The king's answer—"I do them grant and promise."
"Do you grant to hold and keep the laws and rightful customs which the commonalty of your realm shall have chosen, and to maintain and enforce them to the honor of God after your power?"
The king's answer—"I this do grant and promise."

I shall not dwell upon the event most frequently quoted with reference to the era of the Plantagenets—I mean King John's "Magna Charta." It was more social than territorial, and tended to limit the power of the Crown, and to increase that of the barons. The Plantagenets had not begun to call Commons to the House of Lords. The issue of writs was confined to those who were barons-by-tenure, the *patricians* of the Norman period. The creation of *nobles* was the invention of a later age. The baron feasted in his hall, while the slave grovelled in his cabin. Bracton, the famous lawyer of the time of Henry III., says: "All the goods a slave acquired belonged to his master, who could take them from him whenever he pleased," therefore a man could not purchase his own freedom. "In the same year, 1283," says the Annals of Dunstable, "we sold our slave by birth, William Pyke, and all his family, and received one mark from the buyer." The only hope for the slave was, to try and get into one of the walled towns, when he became free. Until the Wars of the Roses, these serfs were greatly harassed by their owners.

In the reign of Edward I., efforts were made to prevent the alienation of land by those who received it from the Norman sovereigns. The statute of mortmain was passed to restrain the giving of lands to the Church, the statute *de donis* to prevent alienation to laymen. The former declares:

"That whereas religious men had entered into the fees of other men, without license and will of the chief lord, and sometimes appropriating and buying, and sometimes receiving them of gift of others, whereby the services that are due of such fee, and which, in the beginning, were provided for the defence of the realm, are wrongfully withdrawn, and the chief lord do lose the escheats of the same (the primer seizin on each life that dropped); it therefore enacts: That any such lands were forfeited to the lord of the fee; and if he did not take it within twelve months, it should be forfeited to the king, who shall enfeoff other therein by certain services to be done for us for the defence of the realm."

Another act, the 6th Edward I., cap. 3, provides:

"That alienation by the tenant in courtesy was void, and the heir was entitled to succeed to his mother's property, notwithstanding the act of his father."

The 13th Edward I., cap. 41, enacts:

"That if the abbot, priors, and keepers of hospitals, and other religious houses, aliened their land they should be seized upon by the king."

The 13th Edward I., cap. 1, *de donis conditionalitiis*, provided:

"*That tenements given to a man, and the heirs of his body, should, at all events, go to the issue, if there were any; or, if there were none, should revert to the donor.*"

But while the fiefs of the Crown were forbidden to alien their lands, the *freemen*, whose lands were Odhal (noble) and of Saxon descent, the inheritance of which was guaranteed to them by 55 William I. (*ante*, p. 13), were empowered to sell their estates by the statute called *Quia Emptores* (6 Edward I.). It enacts:

"That from henceforth it shall be lawful to every *freeman* to sell, at his own pleasure, his lands and tenements, or part of them: so that the feoffee shall hold the same lands and tenements of the chief lord of the fee by such customs as his feoffee held before."

The scope of these laws was altered in the reign of Edward III. That monarch, in view of his intended invasion of France, secured the adhesion of the landowners, by giving them power to raise money upon and alien their estates. The permission was as follows, 1 Edward III., cap. 12:

"Whereas divers people of the realm complain themselves to be grieved because that lands and tenements which be holden of the king in chief, and aliened without license, have been seized into the king's hand, and holden as forfeit: (2.) The king shall not hold them as forfeit in such case, but will and grant from henceforth of such lands and tenements so aliened, there shall be reasonable fine taken in chancery by due process."

1 Edward III., cap. 13:

"Whereas divers have complained that they be grieved by reason of purchasing of lands and tenements, which have been holden of the king's progenitors that now is, as of honors; and the same lands have been taken into the king's hands, as though they had been holden in chief of the king as of his crown: (2.) The king will that from henceforth no man be grieved by any such purchase."

De Lolme, chap. iii., sec. 3, remarks on these laws that they took from the king all power of preventing alienation or of purchase. They left him the reversionary right on the failure of heirs.

These changes in the relative power of the sovereign and the nobles took place to enable Edward to enter upon the conquest of France; but that monarch conferred a power upon the barons, which was used to the detriment of his descendants, and led to the dethronement of the Plantagenets.

The line of demarcation between the two sets of titles, those derived through the Anglo-Saxon laws and those derived through the grants of the Norman sovereigns, was gradually being effaced. The people looked back to the laws of Edward the Confessor, and forced them upon Edward II. But after passing the laws which prevented *nobles* from selling, and empowering *freemen* to do so, Edward III. found it needful to assert his claims to the entire land of England, and enacted in the twenty-fourth year of his reign:

"*That the king is the universal lord and original proprietor of all land in his kingdom; and that no man doth, or can possess, any part* of *it but what has mediately or immediately been derived as a gift from him to be held on feodal service.*"

Those who obtained gifts of land, only held or had the use of them; the ownership rested in the Crown. Feodal service, the maintenance of armed men, and the bringing them into the field, was the rent paid.

The wealth which came into England after the conquest of France influenced all classes, but none more than the family of the king. His own example seems to have affected his descendants. The invasion of France and the captivity of its king reappear in the invasion of England by Henry IV., and the capture and dethronement of Richard II. The prosperity of England during the reign of Edward had passed away in that of his grandson. Very great distress pervaded the land, and it led to efforts to get rid of villeinage. The 1st Richard II. recites:

"That grievous complaints had been made to the Lords and Commons, that villeins and land tenants daily withdraw into cities and towns, and a special commission was appointed to hear the case, and decide thereon."

The complaint was renewed, and appears in Act 9 Richard II., cap. 2:

"Whereas divers villeins and serfs, as well of the great Lords as of other people, as well spiritual as temporal, do fly within the cities, towns, and places enfranched, as the city of London, and other like, and do feign divers suits against their Lords, to the intent to make them free by the answer of the Lords, it is accorded and assented that the Lords and others shall not be forebound of their villeins, because of the answer of the Lords."

Serfdom or slavery may have existed previous to the Anglo-Saxon invasion, but I am disposed to think that the Saxons, the Jutes, and the Angles reduced the inhabitants of the lands which they conquered, into serfdom. The history of that period shows that men, women, and children were constantly sold, and that there were established markets. One at Bristol, which was frequented by Irish buyers, was put down, owing to the remonstrance of the bishop. After the Norman invasion the name of *Villein*, a person attached to the *villa*, was given to the serfs. The *village* was their residence. Occasional instances of *enfranchisement* took place; the word signified being made free, and at that time every *freeman* was entitled to a vote. The word *enfranchise* has latterly come to bear a different meaning, and to apply solely to the possession of a vote, but it originally meant the elevation of a *serf* into the condition of a *freeman*. The act of enfranchisement was a public ceremony usually performed at the church door. The last act of ownership performed by the master was the piercing of the right ear with an awl. Many serfs fled into the towns, where they were enfranchised and became freemen.

The disaffection of the common people increased; they were borne down with oppression. They struggled against their masters, and tried to secure their personal liberty, and the freedom of their land. The population rose in masses in the reign of Richard II., and demanded—

1st. The total abolition of slavery for themselves and their children forever;

2d. The reduction of the rent of good land to 4*d.* per acre;

3d. The right of buying and selling, like other men, in markets and fairs;

4th. The pardon of all offences.

The monarch acted upon insidious advice; he spoke them fair at first, to gain time, but did not fulfil his promises. Ultimately the people gained part of their demands. To limit or defeat them, an act was passed, fixing the wages of laborers to 4*d.* per day, with meat and drink, or 6*d.* per day, without meat and drink, and others in proportion; but with the proviso, that if any one refused to serve or labor on these terms, every justice was at liberty to send him to jail, there to remain until he gave security to serve and labor as by law required. A subsequent act prevents their being employed by the week, or paid for holidays.

Previous to this period, the major barons and great lords tilled their land by serfs, and had very large flocks and herds of cattle. On the death of the Bishop of Winchester, 1367, his executors delivered to Bishop Wykeham, his successor in the see, the following: 127 draught horses, 1556 head of cattle, 3876 wedders, 4777 ewes, and 3541 lambs. Tillage was neglected; and in 1314 there was a severe dearth; wheat sold at a price equal to £30 per quarter, the brewing of ale was discontinued by proclamation, in order "to prevent those of middle rank from perishing for want of food."

The dissensions among the descendants of Edward III. as to the right to the Crown aided the nobles in their efforts to make their estates hereditary, and the civil wars which afflicted the nation tended to promote that object. Kings were crowned and discrowned at the will of the nobles, who compelled the freemen to part with their small estates. The oligarchy dictated to the Crown, and oppressed and kept down the freemen. The nobles allied themselves with the serfs, who were manumitted that they might serve as soldiers in the conflicting armies.

From the Conquest to the time of Richard II., only barons-by-tenure, the descendants of the companions of the Conqueror, were invited by writ to Parliament. That monarch made an innovation, and invited others who were not barons-by-tenure. The first dukedom was created the 11th of Edward III., and the first viscount the 18th Henry VI.

Edward IV. seized upon the lands granted by former kings, and gave them to his own followers, and thus created a feeling of uneasiness in the minds of the nobility, and paved the way for the events which were accomplished by a succeeding dynasty. The decision in the Taltarum case opened the question of succession; and Edward's efforts to put down retainers was the precursor of the Tudor policy.

We have a picture of the state of society in the reign of Edward IV. in the Paston Memoirs, written by Margaret Paston. Her husband, John Paston, was heir to Sir John Fastolf. He was bound by the will to establish in Caister

Castle, Fastolf's own mansion, a college of religious men to pray for his benefactor's soul. But in those days might was right, and the Duke of Norfolk, fancying that he should like the house for himself, quietly took possession of it. At that time, Edward was just seated on the throne, and Edward had just been reported to Paston to have said in reference to another suit, that

"He would be your good lord therein as he would to the poorest man in England. He would hold with you in your right; and as for favor, he will not be understood that he shall show favor more to one man to another, not to one in England."

This was a true expression of the king's intentions. But either he was changeable in his moods, or during these early years he was hardly settled enough on the throne always to be able to carry out his wishes. This time, however, in some way or another, the great duke was reduced to submission, and Caister was restored to Paston.

In 1465 a new claimant appeared; and claimants, though as troublesome in the fifteenth as the nineteenth century, proceeded in a different fashion. This time it was the Duke of Suffolk, who asserted a right to the manor of Drayton in his own name, and who had bought up the assumed rights of another person to the manor of Hellesdon. John Paston was away, and his wife had to bear the brunt. An attempt to levy rent at Drayton was followed by a threat from the duke's men, that if her servants "ventured to take any further distresses at Drayton, even if it were but of the value of a pin, they would take the value of an ox in Hellesdon."

Paston and the duke alike professed to be under the law. But each was anxious to retain that possession which in those days seems really to have been nine points of the law. The duke got hold of Drayton, while Hellesdon was held for Paston. One day Paston's men made a raid upon Drayton, and carried off seventy-seven head of cattle. Another day the duke's bailiff came to Hellesdon with 300 men to see if the place were assailable. Two servants of Paston, attempting to keep a court at Drayton in their master's name, were carried off by force. At last the duke mustered his retainers and marched against Hellesdon. The garrison, too weak to resist, at once surrendered.

"The duke's men took possession, and set John Paston's own tenants to work, very much against their wills, to destroy the mansion and break down the walls of the lodge, while they themselves ransacked the church, turned out the parson, and spoiled the images. They also pillaged very completely every house in the village. As for John Paston's own place, they stripped it completely bare; and whatever there was of lead, brass, pewter, iron, doors or gates, or other things that they could not conveniently carry off, they hacked and hewed them to pieces. The duke rode through Hellesdon to Drayton the following day, while his men were still busy completing the wreck of destruction by the demolition of the lodge. The wreck of the building, with the rents they made in its walls, is visible even now" (Introd. xxxv.).

The meaning of all this is evident. We have before us a state of society in which the anarchical element is predominant. But it is not pure anarchy. The nobles were determined to reduce the middle classes to vassalage.

The reign of the Plantagenets witnessed the elevation of the nobility. The descendants of the Norman barons menaced, and sometimes proved too powerful for the Crown. In such reigns as those of Edward I., Edward III., and Henry V., the sovereigns held their own; but in those of John, Edward II., and Henry VI., the barons triumphed. The power wielded by the first Edward fell from the feeble grasp of his son and successor. The beneficent rule of Edward III. was followed by the anarchy of Richard II. Success led to excess. The triumphant party thinned the ranks of its opponents, and in turn experienced the same fate. The fierce struggle of the Red and White Roses weakened each. Guy, Earl of Warwick, "the king-maker," sank overpowered on the field of Tewkesbury, and with him perished many of the most powerful of the nobles. The jealousy of Richard III. swept away his own friends, and the bloody contest on Bosworth field destroyed the flower of the nobility. The sun of the Plantagenets went down, leaving the country weak and impoverished, from a contest in which the barons sought to establish their own power, to the detriment alike of the Crown and the freemen. The latter might have exclaimed:

"Till half a patriot, half a coward, grown,
We fly from meaner tyrants to the throne."

The long contest terminated in the defeat alike of the Crown and the nobles, but the nation suffered severely from the struggle.

The rule of this family proved fatal to the interest of a most important class, whose rights were jealously guarded by the Normans. The *Liberi Homines*, the freemen, who were *Odhal* occupiers, holding *in capite* from the sovereign, nearly disappeared in the Wars of the Roses. Monarchs who owed their crown to the favor of the nobles were too weak to uphold the rights of those who held directly from the Crown, and who, in their isolation, were almost powerless.

The term *freeman*, originally one of the noblest in the land, disappeared in relation to urban tenures, and was applied solely to the personal rights of civic burghers; instead thereof arose the term *freeholder* from *free hold*, which was originally a grant *free* from all rent, and only burdened with military service. The term was subsequently applied to land held for leases for lives as contradistinguished from leases for years, the latter being deemed *base* tenures, and insufficient to qualify a man to vote; the theory being that no man was free whose tenure could be disturbed during his life. Though the *Liberi Homines* or freemen were, as a class, overborne in this struggle, and reduced to vassalage, yet their descendants were able, under the leadership of Cromwell, to regain some of the rights and influence of which they had been despoiled under the Plantagenets.

Fortescue, Lord Chief-Justice to Henry VI., thus describes the condition of the English people:

"They drunk no water, unless it be that some for devotion, and upon a rule of penance, do abstain from other drink. They eat plentifully of all kinds of flesh and fish. They wear woollen cloth in all their apparel. They have abundance of bed covering in their houses, and all other woollen stuff. They have great store of all implements of household. They are plentifully furnished with all instruments of husbandry, and all other things that are requisite to the accomplishment of a great and wealthy life, according to their estates and degrees."

This flattering picture is not supported by the existing disaffection and the repeated applications for redress from the serfs and the smaller farmers, and the simple fact that the population had increased under the Normans—a period of 88 years—from 2,150,000 to 3,350,000, while under the Plantagenets—a period of 300 years—it only increased to 4,000,000, the addition to the population in that period being only 650,000. The average increase in the former period was nearly 14,000 per annum, while in the latter it did not much exceed 2000 per annum. This goes far to prove the evil from civil wars, and the oppression of the oligarchy.

### VI. THE TUDORS.

The protracted struggle of the Plantagenets left the nation in a state of exhaustion. The nobles had absorbed the lands of the *freemen*, and had thus broken the backbone of society. They had then entered upon a contest with the Crown to increase their own power; and to effect their selfish objects, set up puppets, and ranged under conflicting banners, but the Nemesis followed. The Wars of the Roses destroyed their own power, and weakened their influence, by sweeping away the heads of the principal families. The ambition of the nobles failed of its object, when "the last of the barons" lay gory in his blood on the field of Tewkesbury. The wars were, however, productive of one national benefit, in virtually ending the state of serfdom to which the aborigines were reduced by the *Scandinavian* invasion. The exhaustion of the nation prepared the way to changes of a most radical character, and the reigns of the Tudors are characterized by greater innovations and more striking alterations than even those which followed the accession of the Normans.

Henry of Richmond came out of the field of Bosworth a victor, and ascended the throne of a nation whose leading nobles had been swept away. The sword had vied with the axe. Henry VII. was prudent and cunning; and in the absence of any preponderating oligarchical influence, planted the heel of the sovereign upon the necks of the nobles. He succeeded where the Plantagenets had failed. His accession became the advent of a series of measures which altered most materially the system of landholding. The Wars of the Roses showed that the power of the nobles was too great for the comfort of the monarch. The decision in Taltarum's case, in the reign of Edward IV., affected the entire system of entail. Land, partly freed from restrictions, passed into other hands. But Henry went further. He destroyed their physical influence by rigidly putting down retainers; and in one of his tours, while partaking of the hospitality of the Earl of Oxford, he fined him £15,000 for having greeted him with 5000 of his tenants in livery. The rigid enforcement of the laws passed against retainers in former reigns, but now made more penal, strengthened the king and reduced the power of the nobles. Their estates were relieved of a most onerous charge, and the lands freed from the burden of supporting the army of the state.

Henry VII. had thus a large fund to give away; the rent of the land granted in knights' service virtually consisted of two separate funds—one part went to the feudee, as officer or commandant, the other to the soldiery or vassals. The latter part belonged to the state. Had Henry applied it to the re-establishment of the class of freemen (*Liberi Homines*), as was recently done by the Emperor of Russia when he abolished serfdom, he would have created a power on which the Crown and the constitution could rely. This might have been done by converting the holdings of the men-at-arms into allodial estates, held direct from the Crown. Such an arrangement would have left the income of the feudee unimpaired, as it would only have applied the fund that had been paid to the men-at-arms to this purpose; and by creating out of that land a number of small estates held direct from the Crown, the misery that arose from the eviction and destruction of a most meritorious class, would have been avoided. Vagrancy, with its great evils, would have been prevented, and the passing of the Poor laws would have been unnecessary. Unfortunately Henry and his counsellors did not appreciate the consequence of the suppression of retainers and liveries. By the course he adopted to secure the influence of the Crown, he compensated the nobles, but destroyed the agricultural middle class.

This change had an important and, in some respects, a most injurious effect upon the condition of the nation, and led to enactments of a very extraordinary character, which I must submit in detail, inasmuch as I prefer giving the *ipsissima verba* of the statute-book to any statement of my own. To make the laws intelligible, I would remind you that the successful efforts of the nobles had, during the three centuries of Plantagenet rule, nearly obliterated the *Liberi Homines* (whose rights the Norman conqueror had sedulously guarded), and had reduced them to a state of vassalage. They held the lands of their lord at his will, and paid their rent by military service. When retainers were put down, and rent or knights' service was no longer paid with armed men, their occupation was gone. They were unfit for the mere routine of husbandry, and unprovided with funds for working their farms. The policy of the nobles was changed. It was no longer their object to maintain small farmsteads, each supplying its quota of armed men to the retinue of the lord; and it was their interest to obtain money rents. Then commenced a struggle of the most fearful character. The nobles cleared their lands, pulled down the houses, and displaced the people. Vagrancy, on a most unparalleled scale, took place. Henry VII., to check this cruel, unexpected, and harsh outcome of his own policy, resorted to legislation, which proved nearly ineffectual. As early as the fourth year of his reign these efforts commenced with an enactment (cap. 19) for keeping up houses and encouraging husbandry; it is very quaint, and is as follows:

"The King, our Sovereign Lord, having singular pleasure above all things to avoid such enormities and mischiefs as be hurtful and prejudicial to the commonwealth of this his land and his subjects of the same, remembereth that, among other things, great inconvenience daily doth increase by dissolution, and pulling down, and wilful waste of houses and towns within this his realm, and laying to pasture lands, which continually have been in tilth, *whereby idleness, the ground and beginning of all mischief,* daily do increase; for where, in some towns 200 persons were occupied, and lived by these lawful labors, now there be occupied two or three herdsmen, and the residue full of idleness. The husbandry, which is one of the greatest commodities of the realm, is greatly decayed. Churches destroyed, the service of God withdrawn, the bodies there buried not prayed for, the patrons and curates wronged, the defence of the land against outward enemies feebled and impaired, to the great displeasure of God, the subversion of the policy and good rule of this land, if remedy be not hastily therefor purveyed: Wherefore, the King, our Sovereign Lord, by the assent and advice, etc., etc., ordereth, enacteth, and establisheth that no person, what estate, degree, or condition he be, that hath any house or houses, that at any time within the past three years hath been, or that now is, or heretofore shall be, let to farm with twenty acres of land at least, or more, laying in tillage or husbandry; that the owners of any such house shall be bound to keep, sustain, and maintain houses and buildings, upon the said grounds and land, convenient and necessary for maintaining and upholding said tillage and husbandry; and if any such owner or owners of house or house and land take, keep, and occupy any such house or house and land in his or their own hands, that the owner of the said authority be bound in likewise to maintain houses and buildings upon the said ground and land, convenient and necessary for maintaining and upholding the said tillage and husbandry. On their default, the king, or the other lord of the fee, shall receive half of the profits, and apply the same in repairing the houses; but shall not gain the freehold thereby."

This act was preceded by one with reference to the Isle of Wight, 4 Henry VII., cap. 16, passed the same session, which recites that it is so near France that it is desirable to keep it in a state of defence. It provides that no person shall have more than one farm, and enacts:

"For remedy, it is ordered and enacted that no manner of person, of what estate, degree, or condition soever, shall take any farm more than one, whereof the yearly rent shall not exceed ten marks; and if any several leases afore this time have been made to any person or persons of divers and sundry farmholds whereof the yearly value shall exceed that sum, then the said person or persons shall choose one farmhold at his pleasure, and the remnant of the leases shall be void."

Mr. Froude remarks (History, p. 26), "An act, tyrannical in form, was singularly justified by its consequences. The farm-houses were rebuilt, the land reploughed, the island repeopled; and in 1546, when the French army of 60,000 men attempted to effect a landing at St. Helens, they were defeated and driven back by the militia, and a few levies transported from Hampshire and the surrounding counties."

Lord Bacon, in his "History of the Reign of Henry VII., says:

"Enclosures, at that time, began to be more frequent, whereby arable land (which could not be manured without people and families) was turned into pasture, which was easily rid by a few herdsmen; and tenancies for years, lives, and at will (whereupon much of the yeomanry lived) were turned into demesnes. This bred a decay of people and (by consequence) a decay of towns, churches, tithes, and the like. The king, likewise, knew full well, and in nowise forgot, that there ensued withal upon this a decay and diminution of subsidies and taxes; for the more gentlemen, ever the lower books of subsidies. In remedying of this inconvenience, the king's wisdom was admirable, and the parliaments at that time. Enclosures they would not forbid, for that had been to forbid the improvement of the patrimony of the kingdom; nor tillage they would not compel, for that was to strive with nature and utility; but they took a course to take away depopulating enclosures and depopulating pasturage, and yet not by that name, or by any imperious express prohibition, but by consequence. The ordinance was, that all houses of husbandry, that were used with twenty acres of ground and upward, should be maintained and kept up for ever, together with a competent proportion of land to be used and occupied with them; and in nowise to be severed from them, as by another statute made afterward in his successor's time, was more fully declared: this, upon forfeiture to be taken, not by way of popular action, but by seizure of the land itself, by the king and lords of the fee, as to half the profits, till the houses and land were restored. By this means the houses being kept up, did of necessity enforce a dweller; and the proportion of the land for occupation being kept up, did of necessity enforce that dweller not to be a beggar or cottager, but a man of some substance, that might keep hinds and servants, and set the plough a-going. This did wonderfully concern the might and manhood of the kingdom, to have farms, as it were, of a standard sufficient to maintain an able body out of penury, and did, in effect, amortise a great part of the lands of the kingdom unto the hold and occupation of the yeomanry or middle people, of a condition between gentlemen and cottagers or peasants. Now, how much this did advance the military power of the kingdom, is apparent by the true principles of war, and the examples of other kingdoms. For it hath been held by the general opinion of men of best judgment in the wars (howsoever some few have varied, and that it may receive some distinction of case), that the principal strength of an army consisteth in the infantry or foot. And to make good infantry, it requireth men bred, not in a servile or indigent fashion, but in some free and plentiful manner. Therefore, if a state run most to noblemen and gentlemen, and that the husbandman and ploughman be but as their workfolks and laborers, or else mere cottagers (which are but housed beggars), you may have a good cavalry, but never good stable bands of foot; like to coppice woods, that if you leave in them standing too thick, they will run to bushes and briars, and have little clean underwood. And this is to be seen in *France* and *Italy*, and some other parts abroad, where in effect all is nobles or peasantry. I speak of people out of towns, and no middle people; and therefore no good forces of foot: insomuch as they are enforced to employ mercenary bands of *Switzers* and the like for their battalions of foot, whereby also it comes to pass, that those nations have much people and few soldiers. Whereas the king saw that contrariwise it would follow, that *England*, though much less in territory, yet should have infinitely more soldiers of their native forces than those other nations have. Thus did the king secretly sow *Hydra's* teeth; whereupon (according to the poet's fiction) should rise up armed men for the service of this kingdom."

The enactment above quoted was followed by others in that reign of a similar character, but it would appear they were not successful. The evil grew apace. Houses were pulled down, farms went out of tillage. The people, evicted from their farms, and having neither occupation nor means of living, were idle, and suffering. Succeeding sovereigns strove also to check this disorder, and statute after statute was passed. Among them are the 7th Henry VIII., cap. 1. It recites:

"That great inconveniency did daily increase by dissolution, pulling down, and destruction of houses, and laying to pasture, lands which customarily had been manured and occupied with tillage and husbandry, whereby idleness doth increase; for where, in some town-lands, hundreds of persons and their ancestors, time out of mind, were daily occupied with sowing of corn and graynes, breeding of cattle, and other increase of husbandry, that now the said persons and their progeny are disunited and decreased. It further recites the evil consequences resulting from this state of things, and provides that all these buildings and habitations shall be re-edificed and repaired within one year; and all tillage lands turned into pasture shall be again restored into tillage; and in default, half the value of the lands and houses forfeited to the king, or lord of the fee, until they were re-edificed. On failure of the next lord, the lord above him might seize."

This act did not produce that increased tilth which was anticipated. Farmers' attention was turned to sheep-breeding; and in order to supply the deficiency of cattle, an act was passed in the 21st Henry VIII., to enforce the rearing of calves; and every farmer was, under a penalty of 6s. 8d. (about £3 of our currency), compelled to rear all his calves for a period of three years; and in the 24th Henry VIII. the act was further continued for two years. The culture of flax and hemp was also encouraged by legislation. The 24th Henry VIII., cap. 14, requires every person occupying land apt for tillage, to sow a quarter of an acre

## THE HISTORY OF LANDHOLDING IN ENGLAND.

of flax or hemp for every sixty acres of land, under a penalty of 3s. 4d.

The profit which arose from sheep-farming led to the depasturage of the land; and in order to check it, an act, 25 Henry VIII., cap. 13, was passed. It commences thus:

"Forasmuch as divers and sundry persons of the king's subjects of this realm, to whom God of His goodness hath disposed great plenty and abundance of movable substance, now of late, within few years, have daily studied, practised, and invented ways and means how they might gather and accumulate together into few hands, as well great multitude of farms, as great plenty of cattle and in especial sheep, putting such lands as they can get to pasture and not to tillage: whereby they have not only pulled down churches and towns, and enhanced the old rates of the rents of possessions of this realm, or else brought it to such excessive fines that no poor man is able to meddle with it, but have also raised and enhanced the prices of all manner of corn, cattle, wool, pigs, geese, hens, chickens, eggs, and such commodities almost double above the prices which hath been accustomed, by reason whereof a marvellous multitude of the poor people of this realm be not able to provide meat, drink, and clothes necessary for themselves, their wives, and children, but be so discouraged with misery and poverty, that they fall daily to theft, robbery, and other inconveniences, or pitifully die for hunger and cold; and it is thought by the king's humble and loving subjects, that one of the greatest occasions that moveth those greedy and covetous people so to accumulate and keep in their hands such great portions and parts of the lands of this realm from the occupying of the poor husbandmen, and so use it in pasture and not in tillage, is the great profit that cometh of sheep, which be now come into a few persons' hands, in respect of the whole number of the king's subjects, so that some have 24,000, some 20,000, some 10,000, some 6000, some 5000, and some more or less, by which a good sheep for victual, which was accustomed to be sold for 2s. 4d. or 3s. at most, is now sold for 6s., 5s., or 4s. at the least; and a stone of clothing wool, that in some shire of this realm was accustomed to be sold from 16d. to 20d., is now sold for 4s. or 3s. 4d. at the least; and in some counties, where it has been sold for 2s. 4d. to 2s. 8d., or 3s. at the most, it is now 5s. or 4s. 8d. at the least, and so arreysed in every part of the realm, which things thus used be principally to the high displeasure of Almighty God, to the decay of the hospitality of this realm, to the diminishing of the king's people, and the let of the cloth making, whereby many poor people hath been accustomed to be set on work; and in conclusion, if remedy be not found, it may turn to the utter destruction and dissolution of this realm which God defend."

It was enacted that no person shall have or keep on lands not their own inheritance more than 2000 sheep, under a penalty of 3s. 4d. per annum for each sheep; lambs under a year old not to be counted; and that no person shall occupy two farms.

Further measures appeared needful to prevent the evil; and the 27th Henry VIII., cap. 22, states that the 4th Henry VII., cap. 19, for keeping houses in repair, and for the tillage of the land, had been enforced on lands holden of the king, but neglected by other lords. It, therefore, enacted that the king shall have the moiety of the profits of lands converted from tillage to pasture, since the passing of the 4th Henry VII., until a proper house is built, and the land returned to tillage; and in default of the immediate lord taking the profits as under that act, the king might take the same. This act extended to the counties of Lincoln, Nottingham, Leicester, Warwick, Rutland, Northampton, Bedford, Buckingham, Oxford, Berkshire, Isle of Wight, Hertford, and Cambridge.

The simple fact was, that those who had formerly paid the rent of their land by service as soldiers were without the capital or means of paying rent in money; they were evicted and became vagrants. Henry VIII. took a short course with these vagrants, and it is asserted upon apparently good authority that in the course of his reign, thirty-six years, he hanged no less than 72,000 persons for vagrancy, or at the rate of 2000 per annum. The executions in the reign of his daughter, Queen Elizabeth, had fallen to from 300 to 400 per annum.

32 Henry VIII., cap. 1, gave powers of bequest with regard to land; as it explains the change it effected, I quote it:

"That all persons holding land in socage not having any lands holden by knight service of the king in chief, be empowered to devise and dispose of all such socage lands, and in like case, persons holding socage lands of the king in chief, and also of others, and not having the lands holden by knight service, saving to the king, all his right, title, and interest for primer seizin, reliefs, fines for alienations, etc. Persons holding lands of the king by knight's service in chief were authorized to devise two third parts thereof, saving to the king wardship, primer seizin, of the third paid, and fines for alienation of the whole lands. Persons holding lands by knight's service in chief, and also other lands by knight's service, or otherwise, may in like manner devise two third parts thereof, saving to the king wardship of the third, and fines for alienation of the whole. Persons holding land of others than the king by knight's service, and also holding socage lands, may devise two third parts of the former and the whole of the latter, saving to the lord his wardship of the third part. Persons holding lands of the king by knight's service but not in chief, or so holding of the king and others, and also holding socage lands, may in like manner devise two thirds of the former and the whole of the latter, saving to the king the wardship of the third part, and also to the lords ; and the king or the other lords were empowered to seize the one third part in case of any deficiency."

The 34th and 35th Henry VIII., cap. 5, was passed to remove some doubts which had arisen as to the former statute ; it enacts :

"That the words estates of inheritance should only mean estates in fee-simple only, and empowers persons seized of any lands, etc., in fee-simple solely, or in co-partnery (not having any lands holden of knight's service), to devise the whole, except corporations. Persons seized in fee-simple of land holden of the king by knight's service may give or devise two thirds thereof, and of his other lands, except corporation, such two thirds to be ascertained by the divisor or by commission out of the Court of Ward and Liveries. The king was empowered to take his third land descended to the heir in the first place, the devise in gift remaining good for the two thirds ; and if the land described were insufficient to answer such third, the deficiency should be made up out of the two thirds."

"The next attack," remarks Sir William Blackstone, vol. ii., p. 117, " which they suffered in order of time was by the statute 32 Henry VIII., c. 28, whereby certain leases made by tenants in tail, which do not tend to prejudice the issue, were allowed to be good in law and to bind the issue in tail. But they received a more violent blow the same session of Parliament by the construction put upon the statute of fines by the statute 32 Henry VIII., cap. 36, which declares a fine duly levied by tenant in tail to be a complete bar to him and his heirs and all other persons claiming under such entail. This was evidently agreeable to the intention of Henry VII., whose policy was (before common recovery had obtained their full strength and authority) to lay the road as open as possible to the alienation of landed property, in order to weaken the overgrown power of his nobles. But as they, from the opposite reasons, were not easily brought to consent to such a provision, it was therefore couched in his act under covert and obscure expressions ; and the judges, though willing to construe that statute as favorably as possible for the defeating of entailed estates, yet hesitated at giving fines so extensive a power by mere implication when the statute *de donis* had expressly declared that they should not be a bar to estates-tail. But the statute of Henry VIII., when the doctrine of alienation was better received, and the will of the prince more implicitly obeyed than before, avowed and established that intention."

Fitzherbert, one of the judges of the Common Pleas in the reign of Henry VIII., wrote a work on surveying and husbandry. It contains directions for draining, clearing, and inclosing a farm, and for enriching the soil and reducing it to tillage. Fallowing before wheat was practised, and when a field was exhausted by grain it was allowed to rest. Hollingshed estimated the usual return as 16 to 20 bushels of wheat per acre ; prices varied very greatly, and famine was of frequent recurrence. Leases began to be granted, but they were not effectual to protect the tenant from the entry of purchasers nor against the operation of fictitious recoveries.

In the succeeding reigns the efforts to encourage tillage and prevent the clearing of the farms were renewed, and among the enactments passed were the following :

5 Edward VI., cap. 5, for the better maintenance of tillage and increase of corn within the realm, enacts :

"That there should be, in the year 1553, as much land, or more, put wholly in tillage as had been at any time since the 1st Henry VIII., under a penalty of 5s. per acre to the king ; and in order to secure this, it appoints commissioners, who were bound to ascertain by inquests what land was in tillage and had been converted from tillage into pasture. The commission issued precepts to the sheriffs, who summoned jurors, and the inquests were to be returned, certified, to the Court of Exchequer. Any prosecution for penalties should take place within three years, and the act continued for ten years."

2 and 3 Philip and Mary, cap. 2, recites the former acts of 4 Henry VII., cap. 19, etc., which it enforces. It enacts:

"That as some doubts had arisen as to the interpretation of the words twenty acres of land, the act should apply to houses with twenty acres of land, according to the measurement of the ancient statute; and it appoints commissioners to inquire as to all houses pulled down and all land converted from pasture into tillage since the 4th Henry VII. The commissioners were to take security by recognizance from offenders, and to re-edify the houses and reconvert the land into tillage, and to assess the tenants for life toward the repairs. The amount expended under order of the commissioners was made recoverable against the estate, and the occupiers were made liable to their orders; and they had power to commit persons refusing to give security to carry out the act."

2 and 3 Philip and Mary, cap. 3, was passed to provide for the increase of milch cattle, and it enacts:

"That one milch-cow shall be kept and calf reared for every sixty sheep and ten oxen during the following seven years."

The 2d Elizabeth, cap. 2, confirms the previously quoted acts of 4 Henry VII., cap. 19; 7 Henry VIII., cap. 1; 27 Henry VIII., cap. 22; 27 Henry VIII., cap. 18; and it enacts:

"That all farm-houses belonging to suppressed monasteries should be kept up, and that all lands which had been in tillage for four years successively at any time since the 20th Henry VIII., should be kept in tillage under a penalty of 10s. per acre, which was payable to the heir in reversion, or in case he did not levy it, to the Crown."

31 Elizabeth, cap. 7, went further; and in order to provide allotments for the cottagers, many of whom were dispossessed from their land, it provided:

"For avoiding the great inconvenience which is found by experience to grow by the erecting and building of great numbers of cottages, which daily more and more increased in many parts of the realm, it was enacted that no person should build a cottage for habitation or dwelling, nor convert any building into a cottage, without assigning and laying thereto four acres of land, being his own freehold and inheritance, lying near the cottage, under a penalty of £10; and for upholding any such cottages, there was a penalty imposed of 40s. a month, exception being made as to any city, town, corporation, ancient borough, or market town; and no person was permitted to allow more than one family to reside in each cottage, under a penalty of 10s. per month."

The 39th Elizabeth, cap. 2, was passed to enforce the observance of these conditions. It provides:

"That all lands which had been in tillage shall be restored thereto within three years, except in cases where they were worn out by too much tillage, in which case they might be grazed with sheep; but in order to prevent the deterioration of the land, it was enacted that the quantity of beeves or muttons sold off the land should not exceed that which was consumed in the mansion-house."

In these various enactments of the Tudor monarchs we may trace the anxious desire of these sovereigns to repair the mistake of Henry VII., and to prevent the depopulation of England. A similar mistake has been made in Ireland since 1846, under which the homes of the peasantry have been prostrated, the land thrown out of tillage, and the people driven from their native land. Mr. Froude has the following remarks upon this legislation:

"Statesmen (temp. Elizabeth) did not care for the accumulation of capital. They desired to see the physical well-being of all classes of the commonwealth maintained in the highest degree which the producing power of the country admitted. This was their object, and they were supported in it by a powerful and efficient majority of the nation. At one time Parliament interfered to protect employers against laborers, but it was equally determined that employers should not be allowed to abuse their opportunities; and this directly appears from the 4th and 5th Elizabeth, by which, on the most trifling appearance of a diminution of the currency, it was declared that the laboring man could no longer live on the wages assigned to him by the Act of Henry VIII.; and a sliding scale was instituted, by which, for the future, wages should be adjusted to the price of food. The same conclusion may be gathered also indirectly fom the acts interfering imperiously with the rights of property where a disposition showed itself to exercise them selfishly.

"The city merchants, as I have said, were becoming landowners, and some of them attempted to apply their rules of trade to the management of landed estates. While wages were rated so high, *it answered better as a speculation to convert arable land into pasture, but the law immediately stepped in to prevent a proceeding which it regarded as petty treason to the state.* Self-protection is the first law of life, and the country, relying for its defence on an able-bodied population, evenly distributed, ready at any moment to be called into action, either against foreign invasion or civil disturbance, it could not permit the owners of land to pursue, for their own benefit, a course of action which threatened to weaken its garrisons. It is not often that we are able to test the wisdom of legislation by specific results so clearly as in the present instance. The first attempts of the kind which I have described were made in the Isle of Wight early in the reign of Henry VII. Lying so directly exposed to attacks by France, the Isle of Wight was a place which it was peculiarly important to keep in a state of defence, and the 4th Henry VII., cap. 16, was passed to prevent the depopulation of the Isle of Wight, occasioned by the system of large farms."

The city merchants alluded to by Froude seem to have remembered that from the times of Athelwolf, the possession of a certain quantity of land, with gatehouse, church, and kitchen, converted the ceorl (churl) into a thane.

It is difficult to estimate the effect which the Tudor policy had upon the landholding of England. Under the feudal system, the land was held in trust and burdened with the support of the soldiery. Henry VII., in order to weaken the power of the nobles, put an end to their maintaining independent soldiery. Thus landlords' incomes increased, though their material power was curtailed. It would not have been difficult at this time to have loaded these properties with annual payments equal to the cost of the soldiers which they were bound to maintain, or to have given each of them a farm under the Crown, and strict justice would have prevented the landowners from putting into their pockets those revenues which, according to the grants and patents of the Conqueror and his successors, were specially devoted to the maintenance of the army. Land was released from the conditions with which it was burdened when granted. This was not done by direct legislation but by its being the policy of the Crown to prevent "king-makers" arising from among the nobility. The dread of Warwick influenced Henry. He inaugurated a policy which transferred the support of the army from the lands, which should solely have borne it, to the general revenue of the country. Thus he relieved one class at the expense of the nation. Yet, when Henry was about to wage war on the Continent, he called all his subjects to accompany him, under pain of forfeiture of their lands; and he did not omit levying the accustomed feudal charge for knighting his eldest son and for marrying his eldest daughter. The acts to prevent the landholder from oppressing the occupier, and those for the encouragement of tillage, failed. The new idea of property in land, which then obtained, proved too powerful to be altered by legislation.

Another change in the system of landholding took place in these reigns. Lord Cromwell, who succeeded Cardinal Wolsey as minister to Henry VIII., had land in Kent, and he obtained the passing of an act (31 Henry VIII., cap. 2) which took his land and that of other owners therein named, out of the custom of gavelkind (gave-all-kind), which had existed in Kent from before the Norman Conquest, and enacted that they should descend according to common law in like manner as lands held by knight's service.

The suppression of the RELIGIOUS HOUSES gave the Crown the control of a vast quantity of land. It had, with the consent of the Crown, been devoted to religion by former owners. The descendants of the donors were equitably entitled to the land, as it ceased to be applied to the trust for which it was given, but the power of the Crown was too great, and their claims were refused. Had these estates been applied to purposes of religion or education they would have formed a valuable fund for the improvement of the people; but the land itself, as well as the portion of tithes belonging to the religious houses, was conferred upon favorites, and some of the wealthiest nobles of the present day trace their rise and importance to the rewards obtained by their ancestors out of the spoils of these charities.

The importance of the measures of the Tudors upon the system of landholding can hardly be exaggerated. An impulse of self-defence led them to lessen the physical force of the oligarchy by relieving the land from the support of the army, and enabling them to convert to their own use the income previously applied to the defence of the realm. This was a bribe, but it brought its own punishment. The eviction of the working farmers, the demolition of their dwellings, the depopulation of the country, were evils of most serious magnitude; and the supplement of the measures which produced such deplorable results was found in the permanent establishment of a taxation for the SUPPORT of the POOR. Yet the nation reeled under the depletion produced by previous mistaken legislation, and all classes have been injured by the transfer of the support of the army from the land held by the nobles to the income of the people.

Side by side, with the measures passed, to prevent the Clearing of the Land, arose the system of POOR LAWS. Previous to the Reformation the poor were principally relieved at the religious houses. The destruction of small farms, and the eviction of such masses of the people, which commenced in the reign of Henry VII., overpowered the resources of these establishments; their suppression in the reigns of Henry VIII. and Elizabeth aggravated the evil. The indiscriminate and wholesale execution of the poor vagrants by the former monarch only partially removed the evil, and the statute-book is loaded with acts for the relief of the destitute poor. The first efforts were collections in the churches; but voluntary alms proving insufficient, the powers of the churchwardens were extended, and they were directed and authorized to assess the parishioners according to their means, and thus arose a system which, though benevolent in its object, is a slur upon our social arrangements. Land, the only source of food, is rightly charged with the support of the destitute. The necessity for such aid arose originally from their being evicted therefrom. The charge should fall exclusively upon the rent receivers, and in no case should the tiller of the soil have to pay this charge either directly or indirectly. It is continued by the inadequacy of wages, and the improvidence engendered by a social system which arose out of injustice, and produced its own penalty.

Legislation with regard to the poor commenced contemporaneous with the laws against the eviction of the small farmers. I have already recited some of the laws to preserve small holdings; I now pass to the acts meant to compel landholders to provide for those whom they had dispossessed. In 1530 the act 22 Henry VIII., cap. 12, was passed; it recites:

"Whereas in all places through the realm of England, vagabonds and beggars have of long time increased, and daily do increase, in great and excessive numbers *by the occasion of idleness, the mother and root of all vices*,[*] whereby hath insurged and sprung, and daily insurgeth and springeth, continual thefts, murders, and other heinous offences and great enormities, to the high displeasure of God, the inquietation and damage of the king and people and to the marvellous disturbance of the commonweal of the realm."

It enacts that justices may give license to impotent persons to beg within certain limits, and, if found begging out of their limits, they shall be set in the stocks. Beggars without license to be whipped or set in the stocks. All persons able to labor, who shall beg or be vagrant, shall be whipped and sent to the place of their

---

[*] See 4 Henry VII., cap. 19, *ante*, p. 27, where the same expression occurs, showing that it was throwing the land out of tilth that occasioned pauperism.

birth. Parishes to be fined for neglect of the constables.

37 Henry VIII., cap. 23, continued this act to the end of the ensuing Parliament.

1 Edward VI., cap. 3, recites the increase of idle vagabonds, and enacts that all persons loitering or wandering shall be marked with a V, and adjudged a slave for two years, and afterward running away shall become a felon. Impotent persons were to be removed to the place where they had resided for three years, and allowed to beg. A weekly collection was to be made in the churches every Sunday and holiday after reading the gospel of the day, the amount to be applied to the relief of bedridden poor.

5 and 6 Edward VI., cap. 2, directs the parson, vicar, curate, and churchwardens, to appoint two collectors to distribute weekly to the poor. The people were exhorted by the clergy to contribute ; and, if they refuse, then, upon the certificate of the parson, vicar, or curate, to the bishop of the diocese, he shall send for them and induce him or them to charitable ways.

2 and 3 Philip and Mary, cap. 5, re-enacts the former, and requires the collectors to account quarterly ; and where the poor are too numerous for relief, they were licensed by a justice of the peace to beg.

5 Elizabeth, cap. 3, confirms and renews the former acts, and compels collectors to serve under a penalty of £10. Persons refusing to contribute their alms shall be exhorted, and, if they obstinately refuse, shall be bound by the bishop to appear at the next general quarter session, and they may be imprisoned if they refuse to be bound.

The 14th Elizabeth, cap. 5, requires the justices of the peace to register all aged and impotent poor born or for three years resident in the parish, and to settle them in convenient habitations, and ascertain the weekly charge, and assess the amount on the inhabitants, and yearly appoint collectors to receive and distribute the assessment, and also an overseer of the poor. This act was to continue for seven years.

The 18th Elizabeth, cap. 3, provides for the employment of the poor. Stores of wool, hemp, flax, iron, etc., to be provided in cities and towns, and the poor set to work. It empowered persons possessed of land in free socage to give or devise same for the maintenance of the poor.

The 39th Elizabeth, cap. 3, and the 43d Elizabeth, cap. 2, extended these acts, and made the assessment compulsory.

I shall ask you to compare the date of these several laws for the relief of the destitute poor with the dates of the enactments against evictions. You will find they run side by side.*

I have perhaps gone at too great length into detail ; but I think I could not give a proper picture of the alteration in the system of landholding or its effects without tracing from the statute-book the black records of these important changes. The suppression of monasteries tended greatly to increase the sufferings of the poor, but I doubt if even these institutions could

---

* The following tables of the acts passed against eviction, and enacting the support of the poor, show that they were contemporaneous :

| Against Evictions. | | | Enacting Poor Laws. | | |
|---|---|---|---|---|---|
| 4 Henry VII., | Cap. | 19. | | | |
| 7 Henry VIII., | " | 1. | | | |
| 21 " | | | 22 Henry VIII., | Cap. | 12. |
| 24 " | " | 14. | 37 " | " | 23. |
| 25 " | " | 13. | 1 Edward VI., | " | 3. |
| 27 " | " | 22. | 5 and 6 " | " | 2. |
| 5 Edward VI., | " | 5. | 2 and 4 Philip and Mary, | " | 5. |
| 2 and 3 Philip and Mary, | " | 2. | 5 Elizabeth, | " | 3. |
| " " | " | 3. | 14 " | " | 5. |
| 2 Elizabeth, | " | 2. | 18 " | " | 3. |
| 31 " | " | 7. | 39 " | " | 3. |
| 39 " | " | 2. | 43 " | " | 2. |

have met the enormous pressure which arose from the wholesale evictions of the people. The laws of Henry VII. and Henry VIII., enforcing the tillage of the land, preceded the suppression of religious houses, and the act of the latter monarch allowing the poor to beg was passed before any steps were taken to close the convents. That measure was no doubt injurious to the poor, but the main evil arose from other causes. The lands of these houses, when no longer applicable to the purpose for which they were given, should have reverted to the heirs of the donors, or have been applied to other religious or educational purposes. The bestowal of them upon favorites, to the detriment alike of the State, the Church, the Poor, and the Ignorant, was an abuse of great magnitude, the effect of which is still felt. The reigns of the Tudors are marked with three events affecting the land—viz. :

1st. Relieving it of the support of the army ;

2d. Burdening of it with the support of the poor ;

3d. Applying the monastic lands to private uses.

The abolition of retainers, while it relieved the land of the nobles from the principal charge thereon, did not entirely abolish knight's service. The monarch was entitled to the care of all minors, to *aids* on the marriage or knighthood of the eldest son, to *primerseizin* or a year's rent upon the death of each tenant of the Crown. These fees were considerable, and were under the care of the Court of Ward and Liveries.

The artisan class had, however, grown in wealth, and they were greatly strengthened by the removal from France of large numbers of workmen in consequence of the revocation of the Edict of Nantes. These prosperous tradespeople became landowners by purchase, and thus tended to replace the *Liberi Homines*, or freemen, who had been destroyed under the wars of the nobles, which effaced the landmarks of English society. The liberated serfs attained the position of paid farm-laborers ; had the policy of Elizabeth, who enacted that each of their cottages should have an allotment of four acres of land, been carried out, it would have been most beneficial to the state.

The reign of this family embraced one hundred and eighteen years, during which the increase of the population was about twenty-five per cent. When Henry VII. ascended the throne in 1485 it was 4,000,000, and on the death of Queen Elizabeth in 1603 it had reached 5,000,000, the average increase being about 8000 per annum. The changes effected in the condition of the farmers' class left the mass of the people in a far worse state at the close than at the commencement of their rule.

## VII. THE STUARTS.

The accession of the Stuarts to the throne of England took place under peculiar circumstances. The nation had just passed through two very serious struggles—one political, the other religious. The land which had been in the possession of religious communities, instead of being retained by the state for educational or religious purposes, had been given to favorites. A new class of ownerships had been created—the lay impropriators of tithes. The suppression of retainers converted land into a *quasi* property. The extension to land of the powers of bequest gave the possessors greater facilities for disposing thereof. It was relieved from the principal feudal burden, military service, but remained essentially feudal as far as tenure was concerned. Men were no longer furnished to the state as payment of the knight's fee ; they were cleared off the land, to make room for sheep and oxen; England being in that respect about two hundred years in advance of Ireland, though without the outlet of emigration. Vagrancy and its attendant evils led to the Poor Law.

James I. and his ministers tried to grapple with the altered circumstances, and strove to substitute an equitable Crown rent or money payment for the existing and variable claims

## THE HISTORY OF LANDHOLDING IN ENGLAND.

which were collected by the Court of Ward and Livery. The *knight's fee* then consisted of twelve ploughlands, a more modern name for "a hide of land." The class burdened with knight's service, or payments in lieu thereof, comprised 160 temporal and 26 spiritual lords, 800 barons, 600 knights, and 3000 esquires. The knight's fee was subject to *aids*, which were paid to the Crown upon the marriage of the king's son or daughter. Upon the death of the possessor, the Crown received as *primer-seizin* a year's rent. If the successor was an infant, the Crown under the name of *Wardship*, took the rents of the estates. If the ward was a female, a fine was levied if she did not accept the husband chosen by the Crown. Fines on alienation were also levied, and the estates, though sold, became escheated, and reverted to the Crown upon the failure of issue. These various fines kept alive the principle that the lands belonged to the Crown as representative of the nation ; but, as they varied in amount, James I. proposed to compound with the tenants-in-fee, and to convert them into fixed annual payments. The nobles refused, and the scheme was abandoned.

In the succeeding reign, the attempt to stretch royal power beyond its due limits led to resistance by force, but it was no longer a mere war of nobles ; their power had been destroyed by Henry VII. The Stuarts had to fight the people with a paid army, and the Commons, having the purse of the nation, opposed force to force. The contest eventuated in a military protectorship. Many of the principal tenants-in-fee fled the country to save their lives. Their lands were confiscated and given away ; thus the Crown rights were weakened, and Charles II. was forced to recognize many of the titles given by Cromwell ; he did not dare to face the convulsion which must follow an expulsion of the *novo homo* in possession of the estates of more ancient families ; but legislation went further —it abolished all the remaining feudal charges. The Commons appear to have assented to this change, from a desire to lessen the private income of the Sovereign, and thus to make him more dependent upon Parliament. This was done by the 12th Charles II., cap. 24. It enacts :

"That the Court of Ward and Liveries, primer seizin, etc., and all fines for alienation, tenures by knight's service, and tenures *in capite*, be done away with and turned into fee and common socage, and discharged of homage, escuage, aids, and reliefs. All future tenures created by the king to be in free and common socage, reserving rents to the Crown and also fines on alienation. It enables fathers to dispose of their children's share during their minority, and gives the custody of the personal estate to the guardians of such child, and imposes in lieu of the revenues raised in the Court of Ward and Liveries, duties upon beer and ale."

The land was relieved of its legitimate charge, and a tax on beer and ale imposed instead ! the landlords were relieved at the expense of the people.

The statute which accomplished this change is described by Blackstone as

" A greater acquisition to the civil property of this kingdom than even *Magna Charta* itself, since that only pruned the luxuriances that had grown out of military tenures, and thereby preserved them in vigor ; but the statute of King Charles extirpated the whole, and demolished both root and branches."

The efforts of James II. to rule contrary to the wish of the nation, led to his expulsion from the throne, and showed that, in case of future disputes as to the succession, the army, like the Prætorian Guards of Rome, had the selection of the monarch. The Red and White Roses of the Plantagenets reappeared under the altered names of Whig and Tory ; but it was proved that the decision of a leading soldier like the Duke of Marlborough would decide the army, and that it would govern the nation ; fortunately the decision was a wise one, and was ratified by Parliament : thus *force* governed *law*, and the decision of the *army* influenced the *Senate*. William III. succeeded, *as an elected monarch*, under the Bill of Rights. This remarkable document contains no provision, securing the tenants-in-fee in their estates; and I have not met with any treatise dealing with the legal effects of the eviction of James II. All patents were covenants between the king and his heirs, and the patentees and their heirs. The expulsion of the sovereign virtually destroyed the title; and an elected king, who did not succeed *as heir*, was not bound by the patents of his predecessors, nor was William asked, by the Bill of Rights, to recognize any of the existing titles. This anomalous state of things was met in degree by the statute of prescriptions, but even this did not entirely cure the defect in the titles to the principal estates in the kingdom. The English tenants in decapitating one landlord and expelling another, appear to have destroyed their titles, and then endeavored to renew them by prescriptive right; but I shall not pursue this topic further, though it may have a very definite bearing upon the question of landholding.

It may not be uninteresting to allude rather briefly to the state of England at the close of the seventeenth century. Geoffrey King, who wrote in 1696, gives the first reliable statistics about the state of the country. He estimated the number of houses at 1,300,000, and the average at four to each house, making the population 5,318,000. He says there was but seven acres of land for each person, but that England was six times better peopled than the known world, and twice better than Europe. He calculated the total income at £43,500,000, of which the yearly rent of land was £10,000,000. The income was equal to £7, 18s. 0d. per head, and the expense £7, 11s. 4d.; the yearly increase, 6s. 8d. per head, or £1,800,000 per annum. He estimated the annual income of 160 temporal peers at £2800 per annum, 26 spiritual peers at £1300, of 800 baronets at £800, and of 600 knights at £650.

He estimated the area at 39,000,000 acres (recent surveys make it 37,319,221). He estimated the arable land at 11,000,000 acres, and pasture and meadow at 10,000,000, a total of 21,000,000. The area under all kinds of crops and permanent pasture was, in 1874, 26,686,098 acres; therefore about five and a half million acres have been reclaimed and added to the arable land. As the particulars of his estimate may prove interesting, I append them in a note.*

He places the rent of the corn land at

---

* Geoffrey King thus classifies the land of England and Wales:

|  | Acres. | Value per Acre. | Rent. |
|---|---|---|---|
| Arable Land, | 11,000,000 | £0 5 10 | £3,200,000 |
| Pasture and Meadow, | 10,000,000 | 0 9 0 | 4,500,000 |
| Woods and Coppices, | 3,000,000 | 0 5 0 | 750,000 |
| Forests, Parks, and Covers, | 3,000,000 | 0 3 6 | 550,000 |
| Moors, Mountains, and Barren Lands, | 10,000,000 | 0 1 0 | 500,000 |
| Houses, Homesteads, Gardens, Orchards, Churches, and Churchyards, | 1,000,000 | { The Land, <br> { The Buildings, | 450,000 <br> 2,000,000 |
| Rivers, Lakes, Meres, and Ponds, | 500,000 | 0 2 0 | 50,000 |
| Roadways and Waste Lands, | 500,000 |  |  |
|  | 39,000,000 | £0 6 0¼ | £12,000,000 |

He estimates the live stock thus:

|  |  | Value without the Skin. |  |
|---|---|---|---|
| Beeves, Stirks, and Calves, | 4,500,000 | £2 0 0 | £9,000,000 |
| Sheep and Lambs, | 11,000,000 | 0 8 0 | 4,400,000 |
| Swine and Pigs, | 2,000,000 | 0 16 0 | 1,600,000 |
| Deer, Fawns, Goats and Kids, |  |  | 247,900 |
|  |  |  | 15,247,900 |
| Horses, | 1,200,000 | 2 0 0 | 3,000,000 |
| Value of Skins, |  |  | 2,400,000 |
|  |  |  | £20,647,900 |

about one third of the produce, and that of pasture land at rather more. The price of meat per lb. was : beef 1¼d. ; mutton, 2¼d. ; pork, 3d. ; venison, 6d. ; hares, 7d. ; rabbits, 6d. The weight of flesh-meat consumed was 398,000,000 lbs., it being 72 lbs. 6 oz. for each person, or 3¼ oz. daily. I shall have occasion to contrast these figures with those lately published when I come to deal with the present ; but a great difference has arisen from the alteration in price, which is owing to the increase in the quantity of the precious metals.

The reign of the last sovereign of this unfortunate race was distinguished by the first measures to *inclose the commons* and convert them into private property, with which I shall deal hereafter.

The changes effected in the land laws of England during the reigns of the Stuarts, a period of 111 years, were very important. The act of Charles II. which abolished the Court of Ward and Liveries, appeared to be an abandonment of the rights of the people, as asserted in the person of the Crown ; and this alteration also seemed to give color of right to the claim which is set up of *property in land*, but the following law of Edward III. never was repealed :

"*That the king is the universal lord and original proprietor of all land in his kingdom, and that no man doth or can possess any part of it but what has mediately or immediately been derived as a gift from him to be held on feodal service.*"

No lawyer will assert for any English subject a higher title than tenancy-in-fee, which bears the impress of *holding* and denies the assertion of *ownership*.

The power of the nobles, the tenants-in-fee, was strengthened by an act passed in the reign of William and Mary, which altered the relation of landlord and tenant. Previous thereto, the landlord had the power of distraint, but he merely held the goods he seized to compel the tenant to perform personal service. It would be impossible for a tenant to pay his rent if his stock or implements were sold off the land. As the Tudor policy of money payments extended, the greed for pelf led to an alteration in the law, and the act of William and Mary allowed the landlord to sell the goods he had distrained. The tenant remained in possession of the land without the means of tilling it, which was opposed to public policy. This power of distraint was, however, confined to holdings in which there were leases by which the tenant covenanted to allow the landlord to distrain his stock and goods in default of payment of rent. The legislation of the Stuarts was invariably favorable to the possessor of land and adverse to the rights of the people. The government during the closing reigns was oligarchical, so much so, that William III., annoyed at the restriction put upon his kingly power, threatened to resign the crown and retire to Holland ; but the aristocracy were unwilling to relax their claims, and they secured by legislation the rights they appeared to have lost by the deposition of the sovereign.

The population had increased from 5,000,000 in 1603 to 5,750,000 in 1714, being an average increase of less than 7000 per annum.

VIII. THE HOUSE OF HANOVER.

The first sovereign of the House of Hanover ascended the throne not by

The annual produce he estimated as follows :

| | Acres. | Rent. | Produce. |
|---|---|---|---|
| Grain, | 10,000,000 | £3,000,000 | £8,275,000 |
| Hemp, Flax, etc., | 1,000,000 | 200,000 | 2,000,000 |
| Butter, Cheese, and Milk, | | | 2,500,000 |
| Wool, | | | 2,000,000 |
| Horses bred, | | | 250,000 |
| Flesh Meat, | 29,000,000 | 6,800,000 | 3,500,000 |
| Tallow and Hides, | | | 600,000 |
| Hay Consumed, | | | 2,300,000 |
| Timber, | | | 1,000,000 |
| Total, | 39,000,000 | £10,000,000 | £22,275,000 |

right of descent but by election; the legitimate heir was set aside, and a distant branch of the family was chosen, and the succession fixed by act of Parliament; but it is held by jurists that every Parliament is sovereign and has the power of repealing any act of any former Parliament. The beneficial rule of some of the latter monarchs of this family has endeared them to the people, but the doctrine of reigning by divine right, the favorite idea of the Stuarts, is nullified, when the monarch ascends the throne by statute law and not by succession or descent.

The age of chivalry passed away when the Puritans defeated the Cavaliers. The establishment of standing armies and the creation of a national debt, went to show that *money*, not knighthood or knight's service, gave force to law. The possession of wealth and of rent gave back to their possessors even larger powers than those wrested from them by the first Tudor king. The maxim that " what was attached to the freehold belonged to the freehold," gave the landlords even greater powers than those held by the sword, and of which they were despoiled. Though nominally forbidden to take part in the election of the representatives of the Commons, yet they virtually had the power, the creation of freehold, the substance and material of electoral right; and consequently both Houses of Parliament were essentially *landlord*, and the laws, for the century which succeeded the ascension of George I., are marked with the assertion of landlord right which is tenant wrong.

Among the exhibitions of this influence is an act passed in the reign of George II., which extended the power of distraint for rent, and the right to sell the goods seized—to all tenancies. Previous legislation confined this privilege solely to cases in which there were leases, wherein the tenant, by written contract, gave the landlord power to seize in case of non-payment of rent, but there was no legal authority to sell until it was given by an act passed in the reign of William III. The act of George II. presumed that there was such a contract in all cases of parole letting or tenancy-at-will, and extended the landlord's powers to such tenancies. It is an anomaly to find that in the freest country in the world such an arbitrary power is confided to individuals, or that the landlord-creditor has the precedence over all other creditors, and can, by his own act, and without either trial or evidence, issue a warrant that has all the force of the solemn judgment of a court of law; and it certainly appears unjust to seize a crop, the seed for which is due to one man, and the manure to another, and apply it to pay the rent. But landlordism, intrusted with legislative power, took effectual means to preserve its own prerogative, and the form of law was used by parliaments, in which landlord influence was paramount, to pass enactments which were enforced by the whole power of the state, and sustained individual or class rights.

The effect of this measure was most unfortunate; it encouraged the letting of lands to tenants-at-will or tenants from year to year, who could not, under existing laws, obtain *the franchise* or power to vote—they were not *freemen*, they were little better than serfs. They were tillers of the soil, rent-payers who could be removed at the will of another. They were not even *freeholders*, and had no political power — no voice in the affairs of the nation. The landlords in Parliament gave themselves, individually by law, all the powers which a tenant gave them by contract, while they had no corresponding liability, and, therefore, it was their interest to refrain from giving leases, and to make their tenantry as dependent on them as if they were mere serfs. This law was especially unfortunate, and had a positive and very great effect upon the condition of the farming class and upon the nation, and people came to think that landlords could do as they liked with their land, and that the tenants must be creeping, humble, and servile.

An effort to remedy this evil was made in 1832, when the occupiers, if rented or rated at the small amount named, became voters. This gave the power to the holding, not to the man, and the landlord could by simple eviction deprive the man of his vote; hence the tenants-at-will were driven to the hustings like sheep—they could not, and dare not, refuse to vote as the landlord ordered.

The lords of the manor, with a landlord Parliament, asserted their claims to the commonages, and these lands belonging to the people, were gradually inclosed, and became the possession of individuals. The inclosing of commonages commenced in the reign of Queen Anne, and was continued in the reigns of all the sovereigns of the House of Hanover. The first inclosure act was passed in 1709; in the following thirty years the average number of inclosure bills was about three each year; in the following fifty years there were nearly *forty* each year; and in the forty years of the nineteenth century it was nearly *fifty* per annum.

The inclosures in each reign were as follows:

|  | Acts. | Acres. |
|---|---|---|
| Queen Anne, | 2 | 1,439 |
| George I., | 16 | 17,660 |
| George II., | 226 | 318,784 |
| George III., | 3446 | 3,500,000 |
| George IV., | 192 | 250,000 |
| William IV., | 72 | 120,000 |
| Total, | 3954 | 4,207,883 |

These lands belonged to the people, and might have been applied to relieve the poor. Had they been allotted in small farms, they might have been made the means of support of from 500,000 to 1,000,000 families, and they would have afforded employment and sustenance to all the poor, and thus rendered compulsory taxation under the poor-law system unnecessary; but the landlords seized on them and made the tenantry pay the poor-rate.

The British Poor Law is a slur upon its boasted civilization. The unequal distribution of land and of wealth leads to great riches and great poverty. Intense light produces deep shade. Nowhere else but in wealthy England do God's creatures die of starvation, wanting food, while others are rich beyond comparison. The soil which affords sustenance for the people is rightly charged with the cost of feeding those who lack the necessaries of life, but the same object would be better achieved in a different way. Poor-rates are now a charge upon a man's entire estate, and it would be much better for society if land to an amount equivalent to the charge were taken from the estate and assigned to the poor. If a man is charged with £100 a year poor-rate, it would make no real difference to him, while it would make a vast difference to the poor to take land to that value, put the poor to work tilling it, allowing them to enjoy the produce. Any expense should be paid direct by the landlord, which would leave the charge upon the land, and exempt the improvements of the tenant, which represent his labor, free.

The evil has intensified in magnitude, and a permanent army of paupers numbering at the minimum 829,281 persons, but increasing at some periods to upward of 1,000,000, has to be provided for; the cost, about £8,000,000 a year, is paid, not by landlords but by tenants, in addition to the various charities founded by benevolent persons.

There are two classes relieved under this system, and which ought to be differently dealt with—the sick and the young. Hospitals for the former and schools for the latter ought to take the place of the workhouse. It is difficult to fancy a worse place for educating the young than the workhouse, and it would tend to lessen the evil were the children of the poor trained and educated in separate establishments from those for the reception of paupers. Pauperism is the concomitant of large holdings of land and insecurity of tenure. The necessity of such a provision arose, as I have previously shown, from the wholesale eviction of large numbers of the occupiers of land; and, as the means of supplying the need came from the LAND, the expense should, like tithes, have fallen exclusively upon land. The poor-rates are, however, also levied upon houses and buildings, which represent labor. The owner of land is the people, as represented by the Crown, and the charges thereon next in succession to the claims of the state are the CHURCH and the POOR.

The Continental wars at the close of the eighteenth and the commencement of the nineteenth century had some effect upon the system of tillage; they materially enhanced the price of agricultural produce—rents were raised, and the national debt was contracted, which remains a burden on the nation.

The most important change, however, arose from scientific and mechanical discoveries—the application of heat to the production of motive power. As long as water, which is a non-exhaustive source of motion, was used, the people were scattered over the land; or if segregation took place, it was in the neighborhood of running streams. The application of steam to the propulsion of machinery, and the discovery of engines capable of competing with the human hand, led to the substitution of machine-made fabrics for clothing, in place of homespun articles of domestic manufacture. This led to the employment of farm-laborers in procuring coals, to the removal of many from the rural into the urban districts, to the destruction of the principal employment of the family during the winter evenings, and consequently effected a great revolution in the social system. Many small freeholds were sold, the owners thinking they could more rapidly acquire wealth by using the money representing their occupancy, in trade. Thus the large estates became larger, and the smaller ones were absorbed, while the appearance of greater wealth from exchanging subterranean substances for money, or its representative, gave rise to ostentatious display. The rural population gradually diminished, while the civic population increased. The effect upon the system of landholding was triplicate. First, there was a diminution in the amount of labor applicable to the cultivation of land; second, there was a decrease in the amount of manure applied to the production of food; and lastly, there was an increase in the demand for land, as a source of investment, by those who, having made money in trade, sought that social position which follows the possession of broad acres. Thus the descendants of the feudal aristocracy were pushed aside by the modern plutocracy.

This state of things had a double effect. Food is the result of two essential ingredients — LAND and LABOR. The diminution in the amount of labor applied to the soil, consequent upon the removal of the laborers from the land, lessened the quantity of food; while the consumption of that food in cities and towns, and the waste of the fertile ingredients which should be restored to the soil, tended to exhaust the land, and led to vast importations of foreign and the manufacture of mineral manures. I shall not detain you by a discussion of this aspect of the question, which is of very great moment, consequent upon the removal of large numbers of people from rural to urban districts; but I may be excused in saying that agricultural chemistry shows that the soil—"perpetual man"—contains the ingredients needful to support human life, and feeding those animals meant for man's use. These ingredients are seized upon by the roots of plants and converted into aliment. If they are consumed where grown, and the refuse restored to the soil, its fertility is preserved; nay, more, the effect of tillage is to increase its productive power. It is impossible to exhaust land, no matter how heavy the crops that are grown, if the produce is, after consumption, restored to the soil. I have shown you how, in the reign of Queen Elizabeth, a man was not allowed to sell meat off his land unless he brought to, and consumed on it, the same weight of other meat. This was true agricultural and chemical economy. But when the people were removed from country to town, when the produce grown in the former was consumed in the latter, and the refuse which contained the elements of fertility was not restored to the soil, but swept away by the river, a process of exhaustion took place, which has been met in degree by the use of imported and artificial manures. The SEWAGE question is taken up mainly with reference to the health of towns, but it deserves consideration in another aspect—its influence upon the production of food in the nation.

An exhaustive process upon the fertility of the globe has been set on foot. The accumulations of vegetable mould in the primeval forests have been converted into grain, and sent to England, leaving permanent barrenness in what should be prolific plains ; and the deposits of the Chincha and Ichaboe Islands have been imported in myriads of tons, to replace in our own land the resources of which it is bereft by the civic consumption of rural produce.

These conjoined operations were accelerated by the alteration in the British corn laws in 1846, which placed the English farmer, who tried to preserve his land in a state of fertility, in competition with foreign grain - growers, who, having access to boundless fields of virgin soil, grow grain year after year until, having exhausted the fertile element, they leave it in a barren condition, and resort to other parts. A competition under such circumstances resembles that of two men of equal income, one of whom appears wealthy by spending a portion of his capital, the other parsimonious by living within his means. Of course, the latter has to debar himself of many enjoyments. The British farmer has lessened the produce of grain, and consequently of meat ; and the nation has become dependent upon foreigners for meat, cheese, and butter, as well as for bread.

This is hardly the place to discuss a question of agriculture, but scientific farmers know that there is a rotation of crops,* and that as one is diminished the others lessen. The quantity under tillage is a multiple of the area under grain. A diminution in corn is followed by a decrease of the extent under turnips and under clover ; the former directly affects man, the latter the meat-affording animals. A decrease in the breadth under tillage means an addition to the pasture land, which in this climate only produces meat during the warm portions of the year. I must, however, not dwell upon this topic, but whatever leads to a diminution in the LABOR applied to the LAND lessens the production of food, and *dear meat* may only be the supplement to *cheap corn*.

I shall probably be met with the hackneyed cry, The question is entirely one of price. Each farmer and each landlord will ask himself, Does it pay to grow grain ? and in reply to any such inquiry, I would refer to the annual returns. I find that in the five years, 1842 to 1846, wheat ranged from 50s. 2d. to 57s. 9d. ; the average for the entire period being 54s. 10d. per quarter. In the five years from 1870 to 1874 it ranged from 46s. 10d. to 58s. 8d., the average for the five years being 54s. 7d. per quarter. The reduction in price has only been 3d. per quarter, or less than one half per cent.

I venture to think that there are higher considerations than mere profit to individuals, and that, as the lands belong to the whole state as represented by the Crown, and as they are held in trust *to produce food for the people*, that trust should be enforced.

The average consumption of grain by each person is about a quarter (eight bushels) per annum. In 1841 the population of the United Kingdom was 27,036,450. The average import of foreign grain was about 3,000,000 quarters, therefore *twenty-four millions* were fed on the domestic produce. In 1871 the population was 31,513,412, and the average importation of grain 20,000,000 quarters ; therefore only *eleven and a half millions* were supported by home produce. Here we are met with the startling fact that our own soil is not now supplying grain to even one half the number of people to whom it gave

---

* The agricultural returns of the United Kingdom show that 50½ per cent of the arable land was under pasture, 24 per cent under grain, 12 per cent under green crops and bare fallow, and 13 per cent under clover. The rotation would, therefore, be somewhat in this fashion : Nearly one fourth of the land in tillage is under a manured crop or fallow, one fourth under wheat, one fourth under clover, and one fourth under barley, oats, etc., the succession being, first year, the manured crop ; next year, wheat ; third year, clover ; fourth, barley or oats ; and so on.

bread in 1841. This is a serious aspect of the question, and one that should lead to examination, whether the development of the system of landholding, the absorptions of small farms and the creation of large ones, is really beneficial to the state, or tends to increase the supply of food. The area under grain in England in 1874 was 8,021,077. In 1696 it was 10,000,000 acres, the diminution having been 2,000,000 acres. The average yield would probably be *four quarters per acre*, and therefore the decrease amounted to the enormous quantity of *eight million quarters*, worth £25,000,000, which had to be imported from other countries, to fill up the void, and feed 8,000,000 of the population ; and if a war took place, England may, like Rome, be starved into peace.

An idea prevails that a diminution in the extent under grain implies an increase in the production of meat. The best answer to that fallacy lies in the great increase in the price of meat. If the supply had increased the price would fall, but the converse has taken place. A comparison of the figures given by Geoffrey King, in the reign of William III., with those supplied by the Board of Trade in the reign of Queen Victoria, illustrates this phase of the landholding question, and shows whether the "enlightened policy" of the nineteenth century tends to encourage the fulfilment of the trust which applies to land — *the production of food.\**

The former shows that in 1696 there were *ten million* acres under grain, the latter only *eight million* acres. Two million acres were added for cattle feeding. The former shows that the pasture land was *ten million acres*, and that green crops and clover were unknown. The latter that there were *twelve million acres* under pasture, and, in addition, that there were nearly *three million acres* of green crop and *three million acres* of clover. The addition to the cattle-feeding land was eight million acres ; yet the number of cattle in 1696 was 4,500,000, and in 1874, 4,305,400. Of sheep, in 1696, there were 11,000,000, and in 1874, 19,889,758. The population had increased fourfold, and it is no marvel that meat is dear. It is the interest of agriculturists to *keep down the quantity and keep up the price*. The diminution in the area under corn was not met by a corresponding increase in live stock—in other words, the decrease of land under grain is not,

---

\* The land of England and Wales in 1696 and 1874 was classified as follows :

|  | 1696. Acres. | 1874. Acres. |
|---|---|---|
| Under grain, | 10,000,000 | 8,021,077 |
| Pastures and meadows, | 10,000,000 | 12,071,791 |
| Flax, hemp, and madder, | 1,000,000 | |
| Green crops, | — | 2,895,138 |
| Bare fallow, | — | 630,519 |
| Clover, | — | 2,983,733 |
| Orchards, | 1,000,000 | 148,526 |
| Woods, coppices, etc., | 3,000,000 | 1,552,598 |
| Forests, parks, and commons, | 3,000,000 ⎫ | |
| Moors, mountains, and bare land, | 10,000,000 ⎬ | 9,006,839 |
| Waste, water, and road, | 1,000,000 ⎭ | |
|  | 39,000,000 | 37,319,221 |

The estimate of 1696 may be corrected by lessening the quantity of waste land, and thus bringing the total to correspond with the extent ascertained by actual survey, but it shows a decrease in the extent under grain of nearly two million acres, and an increase in the area applicable to cattle of nearly 8,000,000 acres; yet there is a decrease in the number of cattle, though an increase in sheep. The returns are as follows :

|  | 1696. | 1800. | 1874. |
|---|---|---|---|
| Cattle, | 4,500,000 | 2,852,428 | 4,305,440 |
| Sheep, | 11,000,000 | 26,148,000 | 19,859,758 |
| Pigs, | 2,000,000 | (not given) | 2,058,791 |

*per se*, followed by an increase of meat. If the area under grain were increased, it would be preceded by an increase in the growth of turnips, and followed by a greater growth of clover; and these cattle-feeding products would materially add to the meat supply.

A most important change in the system of landholding was effected by the spread of RAILWAYS. It was brought about by the influence of the trading as opposed to the landlord class. In their inception they did not appear likely to effect any great alteration in the land laws. The shareholders had no compulsory power of purchase, hence enormous sums were paid for the land required; but as the system extended, Parliament asserted the ownership of the nation, over land in the possession of the individual. Acting on the idea that no man was more than a tenant, the state took the land from the occupier, as well as the tenant-in-fee, and gave it, not at their own price, but an assessed value, to the partners in a railway who traded for their mutual benefit, yet as they offered to convey travellers and goods at a quicker rate than on the ordinary roads, the state enabled them to acquire land by compulsion. A general act, the Land Clauses Act, was passed in 1846, which gives privileges with regard to the acqusition of land to the promoters of such works as railways, docks, canals, etc. Numbers of acts are passed every session which assert the right of the state over the land, and transfer it from one man, or set of men, to another. It seems to me that the principle is clear, and rests upon the assertion of the state's ownership of the land; but it has often struck me to ask, Why is this application of state rights limited to land required for these objects? why not apply to the land at each side of the railway, the principle which governs that under the railway itself? I consider *the production of food* the primary trust upon the land, that rapid transit over it is a secondary object; and as all experience shows that the division of land into small estates leads to a more perfect system of tillage, I think it would be of vast importance to the entire nation if all tenants who were, say, five years in possession were made "promoters" under the Land Clauses Act, and thus be enabled to purchase the fee of their holdings in the same manner as a body of railway proprietors. It would be most useful to the state to increase the number of tenants-in-fee—to re-create the ancient freemen, the *Liberi Homines*—and I think it can be done without requiring the aid either of a new principle or new machinery, by simply placing the farmer-in-possession on the same footing as the railway shareholder. I give at foot the draft of a bill I prepared in 1866 for this object.*

The 55th William I. secured to free-

---

\* A BILL TO ENCOURAGE THE OUTLAY OF MONEY UPON LAND FOR AGRICULTURAL PURPOSES.

Whereas it is expedient to encourage the occupiers of land to expend money thereon, in building, drainage, and other similar improvements; and whereas the existing laws do not give the tenants or occupiers any sufficient security for such outlay: Be it enacted by the Queen's Most Excellent Majesty, by and with the advice and consent of the Lords Spiritual and Temporal, and Commons in Parliament assembled, and by the authority of the same:

1. That all outlay upon land for the purpose of rendering it more productive, and all outlay upon buildings for the accommodation of those engaged in tilling or working the same, or for domestic animals of any sort, be, and the same is hereby deemed to be, an outlay of a public nature.

2. That the clauses of "The Land Clauses Consolidation Act 1845," "with respect to the purchase of lands by agreement," and "with respect to the purchase and taking of lands otherwise than by agreement," and "with respect to the purchase money or compensation coming to parties having limited interests, or prevented from treating or not making title," shall be, and they are hereby incorporated with this act.

3. That every tenant or occupier who has for the past five years been in possession of any land, tenements, or hereditaments, shall be considered "a promoter of the undertaking within the meaning of the said recited act, and shall be entitled to purchase the lands which he has so occupied, 'either by agreement' 'or otherwise than by agreement,' as provided in the said recited act."

Then follow some details which it is unnecessary to recite here.

men the inheritance of their lands, and they were not able to sell them until the act *Quia Emptores* of Edward I. was passed. The tendency of persons to spend the representative value of their lands and sell them was checked by the Mosaic law, which did not allow any man to despoil his children of their inheritance. The possessor could only mortgage them until the year of jubilee —the fiftieth year. In Switzerland and Belgium, where the nobles did not entirely get rid of the freemen, the lands continued to be held in small estates. In Switzerland there are seventy-four proprietors for every hundred families, and in Belgium the average size of the estate is three and a half hectares—about eight acres. These small ownerships are not detrimental to the state. On the contrary, they tend to its security and well-being. I have treated on this subject in my work, "The Food Supplies of Western Europe." These small estates existed in England at the Norman Conquest, and their perpetual continuance was the object of the law of William I., to which I have referred. Their disappearance was due to the greed of the nobles during the reign of the Plantagenets, and they were not replaced by the Tudors, who neglected to restore the men-at-arms to the position they occupied under the laws of Edward the Confessor and William I.

The establishment of two estates in land; one the ownership, the other the use, may be traced to the payment of rent, to the Roman commonwealth, for the *ager publicus*. Under the feudal system the rent was of two classes—personal service or money; the latter was considered base tenure. The legislation of the Tudors abolished the payment of rent by personal service, and made all rent payable in money or in kind. The land had been burdened with the sole support of the army. It was then freed from this charge, and a tax was levied upon the community. Some writers have sought to define RENT as the difference between fertile lands and those that are so unproductive as barely to pay the cost of tillage.

This far-fetched idea is contradicted by the circumstance that for centuries rent was paid by labor—the personal service of the vassal—and it is now part of the annual produce of the soil inasmuch as land will be unproductive without seed and labor, or being pastured by tame animals, the representative of labor in taming and tending them. Rent is usually the labor or the fruits of the labor of the occupant. In some cases it is income derived from the labors of others. A broad distinction exists between the rent of land, which is a portion of the fruits or its equivalent in money, and that of improvements and houses, which is an exchange of the labor of the occupant given as payment for that employed in effecting improvements or erecting houses. The latter described as messuages were valued in 1794 at *six millions* per annum; in 1814 they were nearly *fifteen millions*; now they are valued at *eighty millions*.* The increase represents a sum considerably more than double the national debt of Great Britain, and under the system of leases the improvements will pass from the industrial to the landlord class.

It seems to me to be a mistake in legislation to encourage a system by which these two funds merge into one, and that hands the income arising from the expenditure of the working classes over to the tenants-in-fee without an equivalent. This proceeds from a straining of the maxim that "what is attached to the freehold belongs to the freehold," and was made law when both Houses of Parliament were essentially landlord. That maxim is only partially true: corn is as much attached to the freehold as a tree; yet one is cut without hindrance and the other is prevented. Potatoes, turnips, and such

---

* A Parliamentary return gives the following information as to the value of lands and messuages in 1814 and 1874:

|           | 1814-15.     | 1873-74.     |
|-----------|--------------|--------------|
| Lands, .  | £34,330,463  | £49,906,866  |
| Messuages,| 14,895,130   | 80,726,502   |

The increase in the value of land is hardly equal to the reduction in the value of gold, while the increase in messuages shows the enormous expenditure of labor.

tubers, are only obtained by disturbing the freehold. This maxim was at one time so strained that it applied to fixtures, but recent legislation and modern discussions have limited the rights of the landlord class and been favorable to the occupier, and I look forward to such alterations in our laws as will secure to the man who expends his labor or earnings in improvements, an estate *in perpetuo* therein, as I think no length of user of that which is a man's own—his labor or earnings—should hand over his representative improvements to any other person. I agree with those writers who maintain that it is prejudicial to the state that the rent fund should be enjoyed by a comparatively small number of persons, and think it would be advantageous to distribute it, by increasing the number of tenants-in-fee. Natural laws forbid middlemen, who do nothing to make the land productive, and yet subsist upon the labor of the farmer, and receive as rent part of the produce of his toil. The land belongs to the state, and should only be subject to taxes, either by personal service, such as serving in the militia or yeomanry, or by money payments to the state.

Land does not represent *capital*, but the improvements upon it do. A man does not purchase land. He buys the right of possession. In any transfer of land there is no locking up of capital, because one man receives exactly the amount the other expends. The individual may lock up his funds, but the nation does not. Capital is not money. I quote a definition from a previous work of mine, "The Case of Ireland," p. 176 :

"Capital stock properly signifies the means of subsistence for man, and for the animals subservient to his use while engaged in the process of production. The jurisconsults of former times expressed the idea by the words *res fungibiles*, by which they meant consumable commodities, or those things which are consumed in their use for the supply of man's animal wants, as contradistinguished from unconsumable commodities, which latter writers, by an extension of the term, in a figurative sense, have called *fixed* capital."

All the money in the Bank of England will not make a single four-pound loaf. Capital, as represented by consumable commodities, is the product of labor applied to land, or the natural fruits of the land itself. The land does not become either more or less productive by reason of the transfer from one person to another; it is the withdrawal of labor that affects its productiveness.

*Wages* are a portion of the value of the products of a joint combination of employer and employed. The former advances from time to time as wages to the latter, the estimated portion of the increase arising from their combined operations to which he may be entitled. This may be either in food or in money. The food of the world for one year is the yield at harvest; it is the *capital stock* upon which mankind exist while engaged in the operations for producing food, clothing, and other requisites for the use of mankind, until nature again replenishes this store. Money cannot produce food; it is useful in measuring the distribution of that which already exists.

The grants of the Crown were a fee or reward for service rendered; the donee became tenant-in-fee; being a reward, it was restricted to a man and his heirs-male or his heirs-general; in default of heirs-male or heirs-general, the land reverted to the Crown, which was the donor. A sale to third parties does not affect this phase of the question, inasmuch as it is a principle of British law that no man can convey to another a greater estate in land than that which he possesses himself; and if the seller only held the land as tenant-in-fee for *his own life* and that of *his* heirs, he could not give a purchaser that which belonged to the Crown, the *reversion* on default of heirs (see Statute *De Donis*, 13 Edward I., *ante*, p. 21). This right of the sovereign, or rather of the people, has not been asserted to the full extent. Many noble families have become extinct, yet the lands have not been claimed, as they should have been, for the nation.

I should not complete my review of the subject without referring to what are called the LAWS OF PRIMOGENI-

## THE HISTORY OF LANDHOLDING IN ENGLAND.

TURE. I fail to discover any such law. On the contrary, I find that the descent of most of the land of England is under the law of contract—by deed or bequest—and that it is only in case of intestacy that the courts intervene to give it to the next heir. This arises more from the construction the judges put upon the wishes of the deceased, than upon positive enactment. When a man who has the right of bequeathing his estate among his descendants does not exercise that power, it is considered that he wishes the estate to go undivided to the next heir. In America the converse takes place : a man can leave all his land to one ; and, if he fails to do so, it is divided. The laws relating to contracts or settlements allow land to be settled by deed upon the children of a living person, but it is more frequently upon the grandchildren. They acquire the power of sale, which is by the contract denied to their parents. A man gives to his grandchild that which he denies to his son. This cumbrous process works disadvantageously, and it might very properly be altered by restricting the power of settlement or bequest to living persons, and not allowing it to extend to those who are unborn.

It is not a little curious to note how the ideas of mankind, after having been diverted for centuries, return to their original channels. The system of landholding in the most ancient races was *communal*. That word, and its derivative, *communism*, has latterly had a bad odor. Yet all the most important public works are communal. All joint-stock companies, whether for banking, trading, or extensive works, are communes. They hold property in common, and merge individual in general rights. The possession of land by communes or companies is gradually extending, and it is by no means improbable that the ideas which governed very remote times may, like the communal joint-stock system, be applied more extensively to landholding.

It may not be unwise to review the grounds that we have been going over, and to glance at the salient points.

The ABORIGINAL inhabitants of this island enjoyed the same rights as those in other countries, of possessing themselves of land unowned and unoccupied. The ROMANS conquered, and claimed all the rights the natives possessed, and levied a tribute for the use of the lands. Upon the retirement of the Romans, after an occupancy of about six hundred years, the lands reverted to the aborigines, but they, being unable to defend themselves, invited the SAXONS, the JUTES, and the ANGLES, who reduced them to serfdom, and seized upon the land ; they acted as if it belonged to the body of the conquerors, it was allotted to individuals by the *Folc-gemot* or assembly of the people, and a race of *Liberi Homines* or freemen arose, who paid no rent, but performed service to the state ; during their sway of about six hundred years the institutions changed, and the monarch, as representing the people, claimed the right of granting the possession of land seized for treason by *boc* or charter. The NORMAN invasion found a large body of the Saxon landholders in armed opposition to William, and when they were defeated, he seized upon their land and gave it to his followers, and then arose the term *terra regis*, " the land of the king," instead of the term *folc-land*, " the land of the people ;" but a large portion of the realm remained in the hands of the *Liberi Homines* or freemen. The Norman barons gave possession of part of their lands to their followers, hence arose the *vassals* who paid rent to their lord by personal service, while the *Freemen* held by service to the Crown. In the wars of the PLANTAGENETS the freemen seem to have disappeared, and vassalage was substituted, the principal vassals being freeholders. The descendants of the aborigines regained their freedom. The possession of land was only given for life, and it was preceded by homage to the Crown, or fealty to the lord, investiture following the ceremony. The TUDOR sovereigns abolished livery and retainers, but did not secure the rights of the men-at-arms or replace them in their position of freemen. The chief lords converted the payment of rent by service into payment in money; this led to wholesale evictions, and necessitated the establishment of the Poor Laws. The STUARTS surrendered the remaining charges upon land; but on the death of one sovereign, and the expulsion of another, the validity of patents from the Crown became doubtful. The PRESENT system of landholding is the outcome of the Tudor ideas. But the Crown has never abandoned the claim asserted in the statute of Edward I., that all land belongs to the sovereign as representing the people, and that individuals *hold* but do not *own* it; and upon this sound and legal principle the state takes land from one and gives it to another, compensating for the loss arising from being dispossessed.

I have now concluded my brief sketch of the facts which seemed to me most important in tracing the history of LANDHOLDING IN ENGLAND, and laid before you not only the most vital changes, but also the principles which underlay them; and I shall have failed in conveying the ideas of my own mind if I have not shown you that at least from the Scandinavian or Anglo-Saxon invasion, the ownership of land rested either in the people, or the Crown as representing the people; that individual proprietorship of land is not only unknown, but repugnant to the principles of the British Constitution; that the largest estate a subject can have is tenancy-in-fee, and that it is a holding and not an owning of the soil; and I cannot conceal from you the conviction which has impressed my mind, after much study and some personal examination of the state of proprietary occupants on the Continent, that the best interests of the nation, both socially, morally, and materially, will be promoted by a very large increase in the number of tenants-in-fee; which can be attained by the extension of principles of legislation now in active operation. All that is necessary is to extend the provisions of the Land Clauses Act, which apply to railways and such objects, to tenants in possession; to make them "promoters" under that act; to treat their outlay for the improvement of the soil and the greater *production of food* as a public outlay; and thus to restore to England a class which corresponds with the Peasant Proprietors of the Continent—the Freemen or *Liberi Homines* of Anglo-Saxon times, whose rights were solemnly guaranteed by the 55th William I., and whose existence would be the glory of the country and the safeguard of its institutions.

www.ingramcontent.com/pod-product-compliance
Lightning Source LLC
Chambersburg PA
CBHW031551110426
42739CB00039B/1388